The Teaching of Ethics XII

The Teaching of Ethics in the Military

Peter L. Stromberg
Malham M. Wakin
Daniel Callahan

INSTITUTE OF
SOCIETY, ETHICS AND
THE LIFE
SCIENCES THE
HASTINGS
CENTER

The Hastings Center
Institute of Society, Ethics and the Life Sciences
360 Broadway
Hastings-on-Hudson, New York 10706

Library of Congress Cataloging in Publication Data

Stromberg, Peter L.
  The teaching of ethics in the military.

  (The Teaching of ethics ; 12)
  Bibliography: p.
  1. Military ethics—Study and teaching—United States.
2. Military education—United States.   I. Wakin,
Malham M.   II. Callahan, Daniel, 1930-   III. Hast-
ings Center.   IV. Title.   V. Series.
U22.S815   174′.9355   81-86583
ISBN 0-916558-16-9   AACR2

Printed in the United States of America

Table of Contents

FOREWORD

A concern for the ethical instruction and formation of students has always been a part of American higher education. Yet that concern has by no means been uniform or free of controversy. The centrality of moral philosophy in the undergraduate curriculum during the mid-nineteenth century gave way later during that century to the first signs of increasing specialization of the disciplines. By the middle of the twentieth century, instruction in ethics had, by and large, become confined almost exclusively to departments of philosophy and religion. Efforts to introduce ethics teaching in the professional schools and elsewhere in the university often met with indifference or outright hostility.

The past decade has seen a remarkable resurgence of interest in the teaching of ethics at both the undergraduate and professional school levels. Beginning in 1977, The Hastings Center, with the support of the Rockefeller Brothers Fund and the Carnegie Corporation of New York, undertook a systematic study of the teaching of ethics in American higher education. Our concern focused on the extent and quality of that teaching, and on the main possibilities and problems posed by widespread efforts to find a more central and significant role for ethics in the curriculum.

As part of that project, a number of papers, studies, and monographs were commissioned. Moreover, in an attempt to gain some degree of consensus, the authors of those studies worked together as a group for a period of two years. The study presented here represents one outcome of the project. We hope and believe it will be helpful for those concerned to advance and deepen the teaching of ethics in higher education.

Daniel Callahan   Sissela Bok
Project Co-Directors
The Hastings Center
Project on the Teaching of Ethics

v

About the Authors

Colonel Peter L. Stromberg

At present a member of the Corps of Professors at the United States Military Academy, Peter L. Stromberg was commissioned as an infantry officer following his graduation from West Point. He has had normal Army assignments, including two tours in Vietnam. A graduate of several Army schools, he also holds a Ph.D. degree in literature from Cornell University. He is Deputy Head of the Department of English, which is responsible for teaching all cadets courses in composition, philosophy, and literature, and is a former Chairman of the Ethics and Professionalism Committee at the Academy.

Colonel Malham M. Wakin

Colonel Wakin is Professor and Head of the Department of Philosophy and Fine Arts, and Associate Dean, at the United States Air Force Academy. His degrees include an A.B. in mathematics from Notre Dame and a Ph.D. in philosophy from the University of Southern California. He flew as an Air Force navigator for many years and has taught philosophy at the Air Force Academy for twenty-two years. He has written several articles for professional journals and is editor and contributing author of *War, Morality and the Military Profession.*

Daniel Callahan

Daniel Callahan is Director of The Hastings Center. He received his B.A. from Yale and his Ph.D. in philosophy from Harvard. He is the author or editor of 21 books and over 250 articles, primarily in the field of biomedical ethics and professional ethics. Among his books are *Abortion: Law, Choice and Morality* and *The Tyranny of Survival.* With Sissela Bok, he co-directed The Hastings Center Report on *The Teaching of Ethics in Higher Education.* He served as a sergeant in the United States Army during the Korean War.

I. Introduction

This study is intended for military leaders who want to be right, that is, ethical, and who want their profession to be morally right.* Those leaders, men and women intent on developing a stronger, better-reasoned moral consciousness in the armed forces, deserve a description of their noble enterprise—its past, present, and future; its possibilities and limitations. Providing that description, this study sets the stage for the teaching of ethics in the military profession. Ethics, the study of reasoning about moral right and wrong, nurtures the moral consciousness and establishes the basis for right actions by military leaders.

Ethics should be important to military leaders who have a sense of the history of their profession. Leaders of the past have attended to the morality of thought and action in the military. Today's military leaders who are seeking to comprehend the moral dimensions of their work and who are striving to develop the skill to reason clearly about moral matters are not engaged in something new or unprecedented; they are maintaining and enlarging a tradition in their profession, outlined in Part II.

Recently, efforts have been made to teach ethics in the military. Those efforts have been led by people who themselves have seen their lives and their profession directly affected by moral reasoning, good and bad. After the fighting in Vietnam, which stirred the military and the nation to reflect on the moral justifica-

---

*The ideas expressed in all parts of this study are those of their individual authors and are not necessarily coincident with those of the United States Department of Defense or any branch of the U.S. military service.

tion of actions taken in war, active interest in the moral reasoning and conduct of military leaders has increased. Like other professions in the past twenty years, the military has had its old sense of right and wrong challenged from within and without the profession. Its moral reputation has languished. Any hope that the moral anemia of the military profession was a temporary condition vanished in the 1970s when large numbers of West Point cadets, usually an infusion of new, healthy blood into the armed forces, showed that clear moral reasoning did not necessarily develop from learning mottoes, being a young American, or wearing a uniform. The widespread cheating by West Point cadets, coming at a time of troubled introspection in the military, has increased the tempo of the efforts described in Part III.

The following sections treat the actual teaching of ethics today in America's military forces. Part IV discusses a few representative moral problems rising out of the special circumstances of military life. Military people will be acquainted with these subjects, but the discussion may demonstrate some unfamiliar ways of identifying moral problems, precisely describing them, and analyzing and evaluating their moral dimensions. The teaching of ethics, rather than a substantive discussion of ethics, is the primary concern of this study. Thus Part V proposes goals for shaping a teaching program and guiding a teacher through a discussion of problems like those mentioned in the previous section. Announcing aspirations and setting limits, the goals define the activity of teaching ethics and, in effect, describe the state of a successful operation. Since the urge to evaluate progress is especially powerful in the military, Part VI offers some thoughts on measuring achievement in teaching. Part VII, therefore, presents practical advice on techniques for the classroom and some guidelines for choosing the content of courses for the various educational levels in the armed forces. Using the military academies as the paradigm, the chapter looks at education extending from precommissioning classes to senior service schools. The conclusions and recommendations for the future emerge in Part VIII.

The value of teaching ethics in the military and of further developing the capacity for reasoned moral judgments by military leaders seems self-evident. The desire to be a morally sound person is perfectly coincident with another aspiration: to be a fitting leader of America's military forces. The very reason for America's having a military force loses its validity if a ship's captain evinces no sense of moral obligation and decides not to be moral. A first sergeant betrays the military's purpose if his undeveloped moral imagination prevents his recognizing the ethical nature of an issue. A flight leader threatens American values if he cannot analyze a moral problem. A general officer damages the force that he ostensibly serves if he cannot deal fairly with differing ethical viewpoints. The morally impoverished military leader is an enemy of the Constitution he has sworn to protect and defend.

As much as American military leaders may recognize the connection between a well-developed moral sense and the fulfillment of their responsibilities, they must nevertheless confront some skepticism, anti-intellectualism, and cynicism directed toward the teaching of ethics in the military. This opposition manifests itself in remarks routinely made by students in classes introducing the subject of ethics. Some students, for example, initially discount the worth of any study of what ought to be done in a profession that has already established its own laws, statutes, regulations, orders, directives, policies, and customs. But though it may appear that the military's morality is fully defined by these rules, the reality is far different. Military leaders often find themselves obliged to follow rules that can each lead in different, apparently contradictory, directions. They must make a moral decision to resolve the conflict. Asked to make a rule, or issue an order dealing with a new subject, or revise an existing regulation, military leaders find insufficient moral guidance from existing rules. Reflecting on the complexity of life in the military, one quickly realizes how impossible it would be to write rules that specify the right action for all future situations.

The uncertain, unpredictable future, resistant as it is to a comprehensive set of laws, drives some military leaders to the solace of the status quo. They find comfort in going along with the prevailing methods and customs of the organization. People in military service learn at a tender age that the adage "Don't make waves" is a most practical bit of advice. In a profession depending so much on teamwork, harmony, and good feeling, some military leaders conclude that moral ignorance is a leader's bliss. Their objections to the teaching of ethics apparently arise from

the notion that an informed concern for the right may be at odds
with their own well-being. Concluding that "what is" is right,
they have no desire to know of other ways for determining what
they should do. They become prisoners of their environment and
surrender their authority and responsibility as leaders. A leader
without a will of his own cannot claim his title.

However illogical a military leader's desire for placidity at any
cost, a concern about ethics often causes uneasiness, agonized
reexaminations, and painful change. Since people like to think
that they have good reasons for their beliefs, they dislike discovering that they do not have good reasons. Ethics is upsetting.
The study of ethics at its best requires a person to think about life
in a fresh and rigorous way. If individuals in military service
examine their subconsciouses, they may find that their profession
appeals to them largely because few moral demands will trouble
them if they are "straight," according to the military's rules. The
well-ordered society rewards people intent on maintaining its
order and tempts them to march right past potentially disrupting
moral problems. The introduction of ethics into the ranks of the
military breaks the cadence of movement and the repose of fixed
vision. But since leaders can order the right as well as the wrong,
they should welcome the chance to trouble themselves first with a
determination of what actions make sense morally.

A particularly anti-intellectual dismissal of ethics in the military points to the history of interminable disagreement about what
a person should do to be morally right. Not only do ordinary
people disagree, goes this line of reasoning, but generals, kings,
theologians, psychologists, and philosophers disagree as well. No
concord, no value. But if military leaders push this view to its
logical conclusion and refuse to think about all seemingly unre-
solvable subjects, they will have excluded themselves not only
from a study of ethics, but from the study of tactics and strategy
as well, an enterprise that plays and replays battles, past and
future. The analogy is too close to ignore. By studying tactics
and strategy, military leaders commit themselves to uncertain,
open-ended, and problematic subjects. Studying these subjects,
leaders cannot consistently reject the study of ethics on the
ground that disagreement among "experts" invalidates that endeavor.

One of the most cynical reservations about teaching ethics in the military comes from people who think it an act of deceit and hypocrisy. They suspect that commanders have seized the guidon of morality in the hope of laying the venerable flag of philosophy over their self-serving desire for complete obedience and cooperation from their subordinates. Critics imagine, for example, a commander in an ethics class extolling the virtue of loyalty and intending that his subordinates be loyal to him, no matter how immoral he may be. Or critics picture a superior turning a matter of taste—social activities, for instance—into a moral issue. In either case, the critics should welcome an emphasis in the military on moral philosophy. Ethics helps people to think logically about virtues and their application. Ethics helps people to think more clearly about the limits of morality. The rigorous study of ethics helps to expose the kinds of abuses these critics fear. Ethics is the best weapon against the unethical and the hypocritical, even in the ironic case when the unethical person initiates the study.

When ethics turns its attention to the conduct of war, military leaders are likely to encounter an ancient, well-known objection: fighting wars, an inherently dirty job, leaves no place for morality. The cynic simply looks to the past. He sees that Americans have sometimes justified unfair action toward their own soldiers and their allies and have even caused their injury and death without sufficient moral reason. Toward neutral, innocent civilians, Americans have sometimes been indifferent at best and for convenience have placed those civilians into a nonhuman category. Toward the enemy, Americans have sometimes permitted their most primitive impulses to manifest themselves as they avenged fallen comrades and eliminated the threat to their own lives. In practice, otherwise moral American military leaders have yielded to the force of immorality, a force that seems to be inevitable and perfectly reasonable in times of war. Americans have sometimes agreed that war is indeed hell and that in hell they should be at least as devilish as the enemy—and America's enemies are always devilish.

As rewarding as the historical record is to the cynic, however, the past is equally rich in providing examples of military leaders who did not separate war from the human condition. To those leaders who have not denied their humanity because they were fighting a war, America accords praise. To those who have denied morality, it extends a deep feeling of regret for their bestiality.

Since Americans fight to protect basic human values, they should strive not to disregard those values in fighting to protect them. The only way to achieve consistency is to refrain from policies that systematically deny the humanity of America's military forces. Thus, America does not establish rules or follow practices aimed at acting immorally in war or destroying the humanity it fights to preserve. Because Americans will have a chance to commit terrible acts in war, but do not want to behave terribly as a rule, morality has an undeniable claim on the wars America fights.

The teaching of ethics in the military will be useless, perhaps harmful, if it is an empty exercise. Military leaders cannot afford to promote a program they do not understand or support intellectually. They will therefore be well served by recognizing the strong reasons for teaching ethics in the military and by having at hand good arguments to meet various objections to the enterprise. Armed with that sort of intellectual ammunition, they will be better able to formulate and execute programs throughout the armed forces. Knowing the far-reaching reasons for teaching ethics, the military leader will not ignorantly draw on only a single academic discipline for teaching material. Although ethics is clearly a branch of philosophy, the facts and insights about actual conditions of military life that come from psychology, law, history, sociology, theology, and the study of organizational behavior and leadership must not be overlooked. Besides recognizing that many disciplines can contribute to programs in ethics, the informed advocate of teaching ethics will also know that the teaching must touch a wide audience. Since every leader in the military should want his or her actions and profession to be morally right, every leader is fit for education in ethics. In a curious reversal of ordinary expectations, the most crucial students are the leaders with the greatest experience. If at the influential levels of power in the armed forces moral reasoning is faulty or nonexistent, the military and America are in trouble. Commitment to the teaching and learning of ethics at the bottom of the military hierarchy will sustain itself only if junior leaders see evidence of good moral reasoning at the top.

II. Military Ethics—The Tradition

'Men who take up arms against one another in public war do not cease on this account to be moral beings, responsible to one another and to God.' [1]

This insistence on the moral responsibilities of men at war was included in the 159 articles of "Instructions for the Government of Armies of the United States in the Field," written for the War Department by Professor Francis Lieber and approved by President Abraham Lincoln in 1863. The Lieber rules represent one of the two major aspects of traditional military ethics: the association of ethical concerns with the way wars are waged. The other major ethical tradition, which may be distinguished, although not completely separated, from questions of morality and war, is that of attention to the moral character of military professionals.

Moral traditions reaching far back in Western history place limits on the methods of waging war, the treatment of noncombatants, the treatment of prisoners, and reprisals. These traditions also contain moral rules regarding the use of war itself as an instrument of national policy. In Thucydides's *History of the Peloponnesian War* (431–404 B.C.), for example, we are told of the discussions that took place between Athenian envoys and Melian representatives when the Athenian generals were preparing to bring the island of Melos under the jurisdiction of Athens. The Athenian spokesmen seemed to employ a "might makes right" argument, pointing out to the Melians the expediency of surrender in the face of overwhelming Athenian power. The Athenian argument as Thucydides reported it, went as follows:

> . . . we both alike know that into the discussion of human affairs the question
> of justice only enters where the pressure of necessity is equal, and that the
> powerful expect what they can, and the weak grant what they must . . . you are
> not fighting against equals to whom you cannot yield without disgrace, but you
> are taking counsel whether or no you shall resist an overwhelming force. The
> question is not one of honor but of prudence. . . . We are not doing or claiming
> anything which goes beyond common opinion about divine or men's desires
> about human things. For of the Gods we believe, and of men we know, that by
> a law of their nature wherever they can rule they will. This law as not made by
> us, and we are not the first who have acted upon it; we did but inherit it, and
> shall bequeath it to all time, and we know that you and all mankind, if you
> were as strong as we are, would do as we do.[2]

In the end, the Melians refused to yield and were brutally de-
feated by the Athenians, who killed all Melian males of military
age and enslaved the women and children. But while the Melians
could not resist the Athenian army on the battlefield, they could
and did challenge the Athenian argument by appealing to a different understanding of morality and justice. Ultimately, the most
significant thing about this event was that such a challenge could
be made; even at this early period of Western history, principled
alternatives to the "might makes right" justification were available and understandable to the ancient Greeks.

Nonetheless, it was not until several centuries later, after the
time of St. Augustine, though largely owing to his influence, that
traditions of justice and pronounced bans against aggressive wars
were fully developed. Just war theory was developed, not as military policy, nor by military leaders themselves, but by the European moral theologians of the Middle Ages including Augustine,
Aquinas, Suarez, Bellarmine, Vitoria, and the Dutch philosopher
of law, Hugo Grotius. This tradition suggested that if certain conditions were satisfied, a nation-state could be considered "justified" in going to war. These conditions generally included some
or all of the following: the war must be declared by legitimate
authority; it must be waged for a just cause and with right inten-
tions; it must involve the right use of means; it must be entered
into as a last resort, with a fair chance of success, and with
proper proportion to the damage already suffered. The contempo-

rary applicability of such a set of "just war" conditions has received much attention from philosophers and theologians; some version of just war theory remains important to military professionals (especially military leaders) who advise government leaders on the uses of the military instrument and who command that instrument. The consideration of justice in war must form part of the substance of military ethics. It has done so over time through the development of the unwritten and written "rules of war."

In the first half of the twentieth century a number of international conventions were held to delineate the laws of war and to incorporate them in international agreements. Telford Taylor identifies the Fourth Hague Convention (1907) and the 1929 and 1949 Geneva Conventions as the most significant from the point of view of establishing normative restrictions on the conduct of armies in war.[3] The treaties themselves have specific provisions regarding the taking and treatment of prisoners, actions taken in the name of "military necessity," the outlawing of certain weapons, the treatment of noncombatants and private property, neutrality, hospitals, superior orders, and many other issues related to ameliorating the horror and suffering associated with warfare.

In the United States in 1914 the Lieber rules—the first rules of warfare to be formally written down and promulgated by a nation-state to its armed forces—were replaced by *The Law of Land Warfare*, published as an Army field manual and incorporating Lieber's principles as well as many of the conventions of the 1907 Hague Treaty. The most recent edition, published in 1956 (Army Field Manual 27–10, *The Law of Land Warfare*), contains new provisions dealing with chemical and bacteriological warfare. Further provisions dealing with bombardment were added in 1976. The manual at present is based on thirteen specific conventions of various treaties and the "customary rule of war," which the manual compares to unwritten Anglo-American common law. The customary rule of war and the Hague and Geneva treaties function as normative moral rules in the sense that there is no specific international machinery for enforcing them even among the treaty signatories, nor are there any specified penalties for violation. Most nations that have accepted the conventions, however, have incorporated them into their own body of positive laws. In the *Law of Land Warfare*, United States citizens' responsibilities with regard to approved international treaties are clearly delineated:

Under the Constitution of the United States, treaties constitute part of the "Supreme Law of the Land" (Art. VI, Clause 2). In consequence, treaties relating to the law of war have a force equal to that of laws enacted by the Congress. Their provisions must be observed by both military and civilian personnel with the same strict regard for both the letter and spirit of the law which is required with respect to the Constitution and statutes enacted in pursuance thereof. [Ch. 1, Para. 7b]

Other United States written accounts of the rule of war include Air Force Pamphlet 110 –31, *International Law—The Conduct of Armed Conflict and Air Operations* (1976), and Air Force Pamphlet 110–34, *Commander's Handbook on the Law of Armed Conflict* (1980).

As one examines the treaties, the customary law, and the positive laws generated from these sources, it is possible to view them as making specific the more general moral theories dealing with just and unjust wars, especially the classical condition of "right use of means." Though the legitimacy of war as an instrument of national policy in the context of the just war tradition continued to receive sporadic attention from moral philosophers and theologians, the focus narrowed sharply, particularly with regard to "just cause," with the 1928 Kellogg-Briand Pact. The Kellogg-Briand provisions renounced war as an instrument of national policy and seemed to reduce the possible just causes to a single one—self-defense against aggression. The Nuremberg and Tokyo tribunals after World War II convicted a number of German and Japanese leaders of planning or waging aggressive war,[4] and most of those convicted were sentenced to life in prison.

If we attempt to impose a framework on the historical development of moral concerns regarding human warfare, we can suggest a set of evolutionary stages leading up to our present position in which a number of normative constraints are incorporated into positive national and international laws. Suggesting that civilized peoples observe higher moral laws, the earliest accounts of war in the Western world attributed pillage and unnecessary destruction of life and property to "barbarians." The Athenian-Melian discussion reported by Thucydides in the fifth century B.C. pitted "justice" against "might makes right" as foundations for a "law of war" or a "law of nations." In the *Republic*, Plato worked out a highly complex conception of justice that was, he maintained, philosophically and ethically superior to the "might makes right" argument. From Augustine in the fifth century A.D. to Hugo Grotius in the seventeenth century, justice became the dominating theme for those who wrote about war and morality, if not for those actually waging the wars.

During the European wars of the eighteenth and early nineteenth centuries, tactics evolved that generally isolated combatants on battlefields remote from civilian populations, and military commanders seemed to refrain from seeking mass destruction of their enemies. Military leadership of those European armies rested largely in the hands of the landed aristocracy, who supposedly conducted themselves with an inherited sense of honor and followed the chivalric code appropriate to "gentlemen." (More will be said shortly about military honor.) When American revolutionary riflemen deliberately aimed at British officers from behind barricades and natural cover, the British believed the action to violate "the accepted rules of the day."[5] Later, the enormous savagery and heavy casualties of the Civil War in the United States may have been the specific catalyst for the development and promulgation of the *written* Lieber rules. Telford Taylor makes a strong case for the view that the Civil War, along with the Crimean War and the Franco-Prussian War of 1870, precipitated the initial Hague and Geneva Conventions and that these conventions, along with the 1928 Kellogg-Briand Pact, formed the foundations for the actions taken to prosecute war criminals at Nuremberg and Tokyo after World War II.[6] Thus, it is possible to trace the evolution of the moral concern for limiting the savagery and violence of war to the point where international treaties have been signed regarding actions in war; and further, to the point where internationally constituted tribunals have prosecuted and directed the punishment of some who have violated "the law of war."

Another method of analysis might trace the parallel development of moral concerns and warfare technology. The technological capability of war machines today has caused many moral philosophers who might have been just war theorists in another age to call for the abolition of war as an instrument of national policy, even as a defense against overt attack. Thus, military ethics today must examine the thinking of those who concerned themselves with the serious questions of morality in war, as well as the arguments of those who have either attempted to lay down conditions that justify war or argued that no war is ever justified. Clearly, military professionals must maintain some intellectual and moral justification for fighting wars (or preventing them by a deterring military posture) or their membership in the profession loses justification. Those who would teach military ethics must also accept responsibility for promulgating the customary rule of war and the written laws of warfare, both of which are founded on specific moral concerns.

Separate from, but related to, these profound concerns about the morality of war and morality in war are conceptions of military honor and military virtues. One of the earliest statements by an American military figure regarding the need for officers to serve with honor was made (not surprisingly) by General George Washington: "War must be carried on systematically, and to do it, you must have good officers, . . . Gentlemen, and Men of character . . . activated by Principles of honour, and a spirit of enterprise."[7]

That officer-leaders must be "gentlemen" was not an American conception, but even as early as George Washington's time, the inherited European view was being modified. Alfred Vagts has carefully documented the practice in European armies up through the nineteenth century that allocated officer positions almost entirely to members of the landed aristocracy with little regard to merit or character.[8] Vagts was interested in distinguishing "the military way" from "militarism" and he traced some of the least desirable characteristics of military leadership (those militaristic tendencies to glorify war and armies apart from their required political functions) back to the dominance of noblemen in the early feudal age.

The medieval notion of military honor was connected to the privilege of carrying and using weapons, a privilege reserved for feudal noblemen who had a monopoly on the right to bear arms both for fighting and for hunting. As Vagts points out:

Under the medieval formula of the division of labor in society, the knights were appointed to do battle, as the clergy to pray and the people to work. Drastic punishment was meted out to those inferiors who could be caught infringing upon their rights. In 1078, peasants of Southern Germany who had taken up arms for their emperor, Henry IV, were, after their defeat, castrated by the feudal armies for their presumption in bearing tools reserved to the knighthood. The glory of death on the battlefield was reserved for the armored man on horseback; and though common men were permitted to come to his assistance in some extreme cases, this was regarded as abnormal and monstrous.[9]

Diane Bornstein in *Mirrors of Courtesy*[10] provides a more congenial view of the chivalric code, suggesting that it began as a practical set of rules for the use of the military aristocracy on the battlefield but took a romanticized and idealized form in the literature of the Renaissance period. She sees in this code of chivalry for knights an anticipation of the international laws of warfare. Bornstein points out that in *Book of Fayttes* (1489), translated by William Caxton, we find material "on the legality of war, the duties of a knight, the payment of wages, military contracts, spoils of war, prisoners of war, the rights of noncombatants, safe-conducts, truces, letters of mark, duels, trials by combat, and heraldry."[11] She concludes that the "code of chivalry or law of arms" was largely observed by combatants in the conduct of wars during the Middle Ages and that this code had a decided influence in mitigating the inhumaneness of war. She cites the rules against slaying prisoners and against harassing civilians and points to special European courts that upheld these rules. "Chivalry thus prepared the way for the concept of a law of nations in the realm of warfare."[12]

Although *Book of Fayttes* originally was intended for professional men of arms modeled after medieval knights, by the late fifteenth century the chivalric code had been extended into more general rules of conduct for the landed aristocracy. Indeed, by the time Caxton's translation appeared in 1489, the code of chivalry was already receiving less military emphasis and had undergone much romanticizing and immersion in myth. The notion of honor highlighted in the code of chivalry lost the connotation of "military honor" as it pertained to feudal knights; it came to mean nobility of caste more than nobility of individual character.

The ideal of fair play from the medieval conception of honor carried over for some time among the nobles in European armies and presented some grave difficulties as weapons technology advanced. It hardly could be viewed as chivalrous to attack an enemy with vastly superior numbers. The development of the bow and arrow, handguns, and artillery all seemed to introduce an "unfairness" into battle when the knight could not face his adversary directly at close range. Vagts suggests that even through the eighteenth century, the noblemen who commanded European armies were not reconciled to the "unfair" use of artillery; they frequently positioned artillery to the left in battles, signifying its inferior status to the fighting men.[13]

From this tradition of medieval honor some elements of chivalric conduct remain. Perhaps the most obvious is the attempt to maintain fair treatment for prisoners of war. The question of the "fairness" of weapons often arises with the introduction of some technological advance, though concern recedes when all parties to a potential conflict appear equally equipped. The American military, still echoing Europe and especially Britain, continues to count military leaders among the aristocracy but with a difference—indeed a moral difference according to C. Robert Kemble:

> Being unmistakably second-rate in cultural achievements, the new nation chose to claim the superiority of its Puritan-based morality. The influence of this "moral nationalism" on the military image was immediate and pervasive. . . . While patrician virtues like honor, courage, courtesy, and self-sacrifice were looked on with favor, any restoration-styled immorality, any military cliques, or any pretentious trappings were summarily rejected, especially if there was a smell of despotism in the air. . . . Distrustful of potential despots and idle aristocrats, utopian, Puritan, middle-class America canonized military heroes who were gentlemen by virtue of their social stratum *and* their exemplary moral character.[14]

Military honor has remained central in the development of the military profession in the United States, gradually replacing the aristocratic flavor of the concept with both moral and practical characteristics. In 1960, Morris Janowitz described military honor in the American military as "both a means and an end":

> The code of honor specifies how an officer ought to behave, but to be "honorable" is an objective to be achieved for its own right. When military honor is effective, its coercive power is considerable, since it persistently points to a single overriding directive: The professional soldier always fights.[15]

It was to be expected, Janowitz suggests, that the American

model of officership should initially evolve from the British although the American environment produced considerable modifications. He identifies four components of military honor that were absorbed and adapted: (1) officers are gentlemen; (2) personal loyalty is owed to the commander; (3) officers are members of a single self-regulating brotherhood; and (4) officers fight for traditional glory.[16]

Emphasizing the shift in meaning of the term "gentlemen" in the American military setting, Janowitz cites the Department of Defense publication, *The Armed Forces Officer* (1950):

The military officer is considered a gentlemen, not because Congress wills it, nor because it has been the custom of people at all times to afford him that courtesy, but specifically because nothing less than a gentleman is truly suited for his particular set of responsibilities.[17]

Interestingly, the 1975 reissue of *The Armed Forces Officer* provides a version of this same passage that now refers to a "gentle person" rather than a "gentleman,"[18] thus suggesting an even further democratization of the concept.

While personal loyalty to the commander remains an important part of the code of honor, the highest loyalty as expressed in the oath of office involves allegiance to the Constitution and to the position of the President as commander-in-chief rather than to the specific person who is the President. The conception of a corporate body of professional officers remains an important part of military honor, although strains are perceptible here as they are in other contemporary professions. "An officer's word is his bond" continues to be a source of pride in the officer corps, and breaches of this precept of honor still receive almost universal condemnation from fellow officers. But the corporate notion remains strongest with respect to the military's function of fighting its nation's wars: "The most honorable officer is the officer who never refuses combat assignment. To refuse combat assignment would be a breach of honor, a rupture of the sense of brotherhood."[19] The refusal of some officers to accept assignments in Vietnam seems to have reaffirmed this fundamental aspect of military honor. Those who refused combat assignments were made subject to administrative action under various service regulations (some were court-martialed), and only those who made convincing cases for sincere concerns of conscience regarding the justice of that war retained any semblance of esteem with fellow officers. Janowitz's fourth element of military honor—that officers fight for traditional glory—has never been strong in the United States military. The military profession does take pride in its accomplishments and its heroes, but the closest one comes in the American tradition to the notion of fighting for glory seems to have been the appeal of the military profession as a rugged life for noble purposes requiring personal sacrifices.

Having mentioned the traditions in military ethics that are concerned with the morality of war, morality in war, and military honor, we should also take note of certain moral virtues that have special functional significance in the military profession. The notion of virtue most applicable for our context comes from the classical Greek view of *arete*, broadly construed as "excellence of function." The moral virtues, according to Aristotle, result from the excellent uses of practical reason aimed at actions to be done, those actions being voluntarily chosen from the habitual disposition of a person of good character (not by accident or under coercion). Employing this notion of moral virtue, we see that in order for the military function to be carried out well, certain virtues like courage, loyalty, obedience to legal and moral orders, integrity, and subordination of the self to the good of the military unit and nation-state are essential. That is to say, these virtues are not merely supportive of the military mission; they are functional imperatives—military tasks cannot be accomplished without them. Thus, we find Plato in the *Republic* identifying courage as the primary virtue of the "soldier" class in his ideal state. With respect to loyalty, obedience, personal integrity, and courage, he has Socrates say in the *Apology*:

. . . wherever a man places himself, believing it to be the best place, or wherever he has been placed by his captain, there he must stay, as I think, and run any risk there is, calculating neither death nor anything, before disgrace.[20]

And again in the *Crito*:

. . . if she [your country] leads you to war, to be wounded or die, this you must do, and it is right; you must not give way or retreat or leave your post, but in war and in court and everywhere you must do whatever city and country demands, or else convince her where the right lies.[21]

Military ethics has taken into account these particular virtues (loyalty, courage, obedience, integrity, self-subordination) because they are integral to the performance of the military function. In a society like the United States, which has consistently championed liberal values with respect to the primacy of the individual, the military need for obedience and self-subordination has produced strains that can certainly be expected to continue. The task of teaching military ethics must include the challenge of enabling the military profession to rationally understand and accept these "military virtues." Morality and war, military honor, the military virtues—these are the traditional aspects of military ethics that must be taken into account by those who wish to examine or teach ethics in the military profession.

The recent example of the United States involvement in the Vietnam War makes clear that much of our national agony revolved around "just war" issues. Was the classical condition of "legitimate authority" satisfied by the Tonkin Bay Resolution? Was the condition of "just cause" made unambiguously clear? Was "right intention" satisfied? Obviously, much attention was directed to "right use of means" and applications of the law of war. Reports of atrocities on both sides focused attention on the moral responsibilities of commanders and individual soldiers. Treatment of prisoners of war caused us to review the law of war and generated new publications explaining provisions of international treaties. Evidence of courageous acts, false reporting, competent and incompetent leadership combined to call attention to the traditional conceptions of military honor and the military virtues. Events in the larger society at the close of the United States participation in Vietnam (e.g., Watergate, bribes by multinational corporations) provided reminders that moral integrity and obedience to lawful authority have significance not restricted to the military profession. Conceivably, one of the most important "lessons" to be learned from the Vietnam War is that the role of ethics in the military profession needs to be better understood by those who are charged with the responsibilities of the profession both in peace and in war. The moral questions introduced by technology and shifting international relationships are complex, but that cannot serve as an excuse to turn our backs on the teaching of military ethics. Indeed, these complexities dictate a greater need than ever before in human history to intensify efforts to understand and teach ethics in the military.

III. Recent Efforts in the Teaching of Military Ethics*

It is by no means enough that an officer of the Navy should be a capable mariner. He must be that, of course, but also a great deal more. He should be as well a gentleman of liberal education, refined manners, punctilious courtesy, and the nicest sense of personal honor.

This quotation from John Paul Jones is taken from the text of his 1775 letter to Congress. It appears as the first item in the United States Naval Institute's publication, *Naval Leadership with Some Hints to Junior Officers and Others*, first prepared in 1925. By 1939, it had gone through four editions, and it was used in the Naval Academy's leadership course during those years. The excerpt quoted above has been memorized by many new students at Annapolis as part of the initiation rites during plebe summer. For our purposes, it serves to illustrate one form of ethics instruction, namely, holding up the example and publishing the writings of certain military leaders.

In the same vein, General MacArthur's 1962 "Duty, Honor, Country" speech at West Point has been republished in a host of professional texts and has been read and discussed by thousands of officer candidates and professional soldiers who learn from it what he called "the ethics of the American soldier." General George C. Marshall, Omar Bradley, Maxwell Taylor, and many

---

*This discussion of current and recent efforts in the military services to teach ethics is not necessarily complete or up-to-date and may not describe the most recent changes.

other well-known senior military leaders have provided materials that have been used either formally or informally to enhance the traditions of military ethics. In 1972, after the much-publicized General Lavelle affair involving false reporting in Vietnam, Air Force General John D. Ryan issued a policy letter to all Air Force commanders in which he reminded them that "integrity is the most important responsibility of command." A number of military scholars, particularly during the past decade, have published articles in the professional journals of all the armed services dealing with the role and status of ethics in the military profession. These sources—the statements and actions of senior commanders plus the writings of concerned military scholars—communicate principles of military ethics and contemporary issues of professional concern. We judge the corpus of these materials to be at least as large as those generated in other professions, and perhaps larger than in most professions with the possible exception of medicine and law. The production of materials on ethics is not, of course, necessarily the most effective means of teaching ethics, nor does it guarantee that those materials will be read and taken seriously by all members of the profession. Moreover, in our opinion, the majority of military people do not read these materials as part of their professional development and hence are not influenced by them.

A number of book-length publications dealing with military leadership, with extended sections dealing with the military virtues and the moral responsibilities of military professionals, have been issued by various agencies of the Department of Defense. One of the best known was prepared by S. L. A. Marshall in 1950 and published under the title *The Armed Forces Officer*, as a DOD, Department of the Army, Department of the Navy, and Department of the Air Force pamphlet. This book has been issued to officer trainees in a number of programs of the various service branches and, in its revised 1975 paperback edition, is still issued to many Army officers during early training. For many officers commissioned during the past thirty years, *The Armed Forces Officer* has been the principal reference for professional military ethics.

In 1949 and 1959, The U.S. Naval Institute published a substantial volume, *Naval Leadership* (successor to the 1925 small handbook mentioned earlier), which provides considerable acquaintance with leadership traditions and a specific chapter on moral leadership. This text has been used to teach military ethics to generations of Annapolis students and has seen other use in Navy training programs. Air Force ROTC published a volume entitled *Concepts of Air Force Leadership* in 1970, and that volume contains a lengthy section of readings discussing the issues of military ethics. Both the Air War College and the Army War College have printed (locally) anthologies of readings on professional military ethics to support their core lessons and elective courses in ethics over the past several years. Thus, a number of official texts or anthologies published by the Department of Defense or the services contain specific materials aimed at the inculcation of the moral virtues in military leaders. Again we must note that the mere existence of these materials does not provide assurance of any consistent or widespread use.

In 1951, Secretary of Defense George C. Marshall initiated what were called "character guidance" programs in all branches of the service. Some programs, of course, were already in existence, but all received significant revitalization and emphasis with the issuance of Secretary Marshall's memorandum. His directive, incidentally, made the point that the moral development of service people was "the traditional responsibility of command." To assist commanders and their chaplains (who were given instructional responsibilities), a six-volume series of pamphlets entitled *Duty—Honor—Country* (Character Guidance Discussion Topics) was published in 1951 and 1952 by the Departments of the Army and the Air Force. The Army and Air Force programs were called "Character Guidance" and consisted in monthly lecture-discussion sessions led by chaplains for every military unit. The parallel program in the Navy was called "The Protection of Moral Standards and Character Education." These monthly sessions dealt with many topics beyond the normal purview of professional ethics. Among the subjects discussed were honor, sense of duty, personal integrity, man's moral nature, character development, professionalism, and authority. In addition, the sessions dealt with alcoholism, ambition, humility, spiritual development, prejudice, chastity, marriage, and family responsibilities.

The moral leadership lectures turned out to vary widely in

quality with the competence of the lecturer, and they were generally unpopular and ineffective. By 1957, major changes were made in these programs to take into account the experience of the American prisoners of war in Korea and the new Code of Conduct promulgated by President Eisenhower in 1955. The Air Force program became known as the Dynamics of Moral Leadership Lecture Program, but by 1961 it was integrated into the official general military training requirements of all military personnel. The Code of Conduct training consisted in the promulgation and discussion of six major precepts concerning the obligations of all American fighting men in battle and in the event of capture. Returned Vietnam prisoners of war have given much credit to the Code of Conduct training, while their experience has suggested some possible variations in interpretation of the Code.

Formal Courses in Professional and Military Ethics

Within the military services, the equivalent of college-level courses in ethics are taught at some of the service academies and at some of the professional military schools (staff and war colleges). At each of the service academies, a form of professional ethics training has taken place during most of this century, at least through instruction in and living under an honor code. The honor codes single out lying, cheating, stealing, and the toleration of these acts by peers, as special violations of professional military honor. Severe penalties have been imposed upon violators of the cadet honor codes (usually they have been requested to resign), although the administration of these codes has changed somewhat, especially in the past two decades. Instruction in the precepts of the codes traditionally has been entrusted to the upper-class cadets, most often through senior elected representatives on honor committees. This cadet instruction has been criticized periodically because most cadet instructors cannot be expected to be well read in the moral philosophy that serves as underpinning for the honor codes. Occasionally, undue emphasis on case studies and the administration of the codes has generated narrow legalistic attitudes toward code compliance rather than a broad sense of moral maturity and sophisticated moral reasoning. The codes themselves are obviously narrow, but they appear to have been effective in reinforcing general honesty in the character of officer candidates.

College-level courses in ethics taught by English or philosophy professors have been available at West Point and the Air Force Academy for the past twenty years. Initially, at West Point, the semester-long course required of cadets introduced them to moral values through literature. Since 1978, a philosophy course in ethics has been developed and taught with the aid and consultation of distinguished visiting civilian philosophy professors. Army officers with advanced degrees in philosophy are currently assuming responsibility for teaching this required course. It provides an introduction to moral reasoning, a foundation in Western ethical theories, and emphasis on professional military ethics, including the war and morality issues. At the Air Force Academy, an ethics course has been taught by philosophy instructors since 1959, first as a core philosophy option offered to a significant portion of each class (one-third to over one-half), and since 1975 as a required course to all juniors. The present course introduces students to moral reasoning, a number of Western ethical theories, the role of ethics in the military profession, and the different issues involved in questions of morality and warfare. At the Naval Academy, many of the traditions of military honor and ethics are taught in the basic leadership course to all students, and an elective in ethics taught by a philosophy professor is also available. At each of these academies, as well as at the Coast Guard Academy, the traditions of military honor are communicated in many of the professional military training courses and are touched upon with varying emphasis in leadership, history, philosophy, and English courses. As noted, two of the academies have a formal ethics course requirement.

The teaching of military ethics in other programs that prepare young people for commissioned service has varied over the years and is receiving current emphasis. Reserve Officer Training Corps (ROTC) programs, Officer Training Schools (OTS), and Officer Candidate Schools (OCS) have all incorporated some professional ethics materials in their leadership courses. *The Armed Forces Officer*, *Naval Leadership*, and *Concepts of Air Force Leadership*, all mentioned earlier, have provided source material for instructors in these programs. At present, Air Force ROTC students are issued a self-paced programmed text in ethics. The United States Army Soldier Support Center at Fort Benjamin Harrison established a full-time Ethics Task Force in September, 1980, to develop an overall plan that would "enhance Army-wide ethics endeavors in the areas of research, policy advice, concept development, training development, training, and related areas." Such a plan has been published and approved and is being implemented in various stages.

The first major task to be completed was the development of a course in professional ethics for all Army ROTC units. This course package includes a course management guide, lesson plans for instructors, handouts for students, and case studies. It is planned as a twelve-lesson course, has extensive readings, and was taught on selected civilian campuses in the spring of 1981. All Army ROTC units began teaching the course during the 1981–82 academic year. In preparation is a similar course for all Army basic officer branch schools where present instruction in professional ethics is varied and minimal. Other tasks that the Army Ethics Task Force has in various stages of production include reading lists and discussion guides in professional ethics, a conceptual policy document, materials to support leadership courses for noncommissioned officers, support of values research, training of ethics instructors, and the maintenance of a professional ethics resource collection.

In the other services—Air Force, Navy, Marines—most basic officer training courses include some materials dealing with professional military ethics. Typically, these programs contain a few lessons taught by regular training instructors who make use of case studies. The advanced professional military education courses (staff colleges and war colleges) in all of the services include some professional military ethics instruction, but the amount of time devoted to this instruction varies considerably among the schools and within each school from year to year. Both the National War College and the Industrial College of the Armed Forces (ICAF) have had some professional ethics instruction in their curricula for several years. The National War College currently offers an optional two-course sequence: Ethics and the Public Servant (fall) and Ethics and War (spring). The 1981–82 offering at ICAF included nine hours devoted to professional ethics. The Air War College, Army War College, and Naval War College have dedicated some portion of their core curriculum to professional ethics for several years. The typical course offers guest lectures followed by a series of seminar discussions over a one-week period. At the Air War College an elective course in professional ethics has been available for several years, but a relatively small number of officers have chosen to take it. At the Army War College, the elective course in ethics has drawn a respectable number of students for some years. At the Naval War College, Admiral Stockdale, during his tenure as president of the War College, introduced and assisted in the teaching of an elective course in ethics that drew many students. At the Armed Forces Staff College, professional ethics materials are incorporated into the core offerings and normally take the form of guest lectures followed by seminar discussions (typically spread over a one- to two-week period).

Military Ethics Research

During the past decade, a number of students at the various advanced professional military education courses mentioned in the preceding paragraph have elected to write their theses on the topic of professional ethics. These papers are available in the archives of the respective schools. Additionally, the Naval War College Center for Advanced Research sponsored and published two major studies of military ethics, one in 1979 and one in 1980. Both studies, one empirical and one essentially a literature search, provide some assistance for those attempting to understand both the status and the general perceptions of military ethics; and they provide decent bibliographies. Perhaps the most significant official study of professional military ethics done in recent years was the Army War College *Study on Military Professionalism*, completed in 1970 at the request of Army Chief of Staff, General Westmoreland. This study has received considerable attention from military and civilian scholars. It shows, in the perceptions of Army officers at that time, a significant difference between the ideals of professional military ethics and the actual existing professional climate. It concluded that the unhealthy ethical climate was not self-correcting and that there was a strong correlation between conceptions of ethical conduct and military competence. Areas of greatest concern to the majority of officers queried in this study included "selfish, promotion-oriented behavior; inadequate communication between junior and senior; distorted or dishonest reporting of status, statistics, or officer efficiency; disregard for principles but total respect for accomplishing even the most trivial mission with zero defects; disloyalty to subordinates; senior officers setting poor standards of ethical/professional behavior." A similar study completed by a student at the Army War College in 1977 produced similar findings. Both studies stressed the importance that the respondents attached to professional ethics. Other research in this area has been encouraged, supported, and published by the Inter-University Seminar on Armed Forces and Society through its founding chairman, Morris Janowitz, and other dedicated civilian scholars including Charles Moskos and the current chairman, Sam Sarkesian.

Recently a group of officers from the several services established an informal organization known as the Joint Services Conference on Professional Ethics (JSCOPE). The group met first in September, 1979, and has held annual meetings since that time. The membership is essentially constituted of those officers and some interested civilians whose duties or personal interests center on the teaching of military ethics. JSCOPE meetings facilitate the exchange of information on teaching techniques, materials available, and developments in professional ethics programs in the various services. JSCOPE has been strongly encouraged and has received some financial support from military commanders who have served as hosts. The Hastings Center has also provided consultative assistance and has included military ethics in its annual summer workshop on professional ethics.

In April, 1980, the Air Force Academy began publication of a new journal entitled the *United States Air Force Academy Journal of Professional Military Ethics*, a periodical more formal than the Military Academy's local pamphlet, *Ethics and the Military Profession*, begun in 1978. Published semiannually, the Air Force Academy's journal aims at an audience of officers and senior noncommissioned officers. Its purpose is "to serve as an open forum for stimulating discussion of issues that raise questions of ethical conduct for Air Force personnel." Its circulation initially has included only the Air Force Academy and members of JSCOPE.

As with many other professional fields in recent years, the armed forces have seen a fresh interest in the teaching of ethics. Yet the pattern in the military is not all that dissimilar from other fields. Interest in the subject is by no means universal or implemented with consistency. In some commands, serious and sophisticated programs are being developed; in others, very little is being done. In some places, a serious effort has been made to develop suitable training programs for those who will teach ethics. In other places, the training appears casual or nonexistent. While there is a large and developing literature on the subject, not all of that literature meets the highest standards of rigor or seriousness. A primary task now is a more widespread, consistent, and coherent teaching of ethics in the various services and at different command levels. No less important is the need to improve the quality of the teaching and the preparation of the teachers, and to promote greater command support for the subject.

IV. Some Problems in Military Ethics

Professional military ethics, like professional ethics in other fields, is a subset of ethics distinguished not by attention to a particular moral theory, but by the problems and circumstances peculiar to the military profession. Military ethics is applied ethics; its substance consists in the application of normative ethical theories to the decisions and actions of individuals in rigidly hierarchical organizations who are charged with the responsibility of defending the state against its enemies and authorized to kill for reasons of state. Thus, moral questions pertaining to the use of violence and the taking of human life are of paramount concern in military ethics. Such questions are not unique to the military—consider the physician faced with the question of abortion—but they confront the military in unique ways. Similarly, moral issues unrelated to violence and killing fall within the domain of military ethics, not because only military leaders face them, but because military leaders face them in special ways within the military context.

The issues discussed in this section are examples of problems in military ethics. From the wide range of important topics, we have chosen to discuss six—obedience, false reporting, careerism, efficiency reports, protecting the innocent in war, and the use of nuclear, chemical, and biological weapons. That only the last two issues on this list arise exclusively from war is a reminder that military forces spend most of their time preparing for war, not fighting. The moral consciousness of America's military forces develops as leaders train their followers to fight; the cultivation of sound moral reasoning and functional moral virtues most likely occurs during time of peace. Thus, four of the six examples deal with situations that occur in peace as well as war. For instance, all professions face the problem of careerism; but because the urge to advance one's own professional prospects has such special implications when lives may be at stake, careerism is a major subject of great practical significance in the military profession's study of ethics. Indeed, in the military, ordinary moral issues take on a special seriousness because decisions and actions so frequently have life-and-death implications. Leaders entrusted with immense power over other human beings and with the employment of immensely powerful weapons cannot take ethics lightly. The stakes are too high. The following subjects are by no means exhaustive or necessarily always the most important. Yet they provide a good sample.

A. Obedience

The virtue of obedience finds serious support in military circles. Leaders recognize that a military organization will not work unless subordinates are obedient to superiors. Because orders in the military must direct people to perform naturally distasteful acts—such as working under outrageously adverse conditions or risking their lives—obedient response ratifies the military structure. "Obedience," however, has a mechanical, brutish connotation that fits uneasily wth our usual conceptions of moral responsibility. Thinking, sensitive, independent human beings with well-reasoned moral beliefs of their own (a description, one would hope, of American military persons of all ranks, grades, and services) should not necessarily be obedient to higher military authority in every case. Existing laws and regulations recognize exceptions to obedience when an order is illegal. Although refusing to obey an illegal order is no simple matter, dealing with other subtler challenges to obedience is perhaps even more difficult. Bound to obedience, military leaders face moral problems when they conclude that an order is wrongheaded or flatly at odds with their own moral beliefs. And, as usual, sorting out the morally right course of action depends heavily on an accurate determination of the facts and a sound justification of personal moral beliefs.

When military officers are inclined to disobey because an order is wrong, knowledge of the facts and the probable consequences of disobedience is vital. Stupidity and incompetence, though they constitute in the military—particularly the military at war—the ultimate immorality, may be compounded when an order is disobeyed. Disobedience seldom eliminates the source of stupidity; in fact, it delivers to the incompetent commander a weapon for a righteous charge against the disobedient. A subordinate must further recognize that the wrong order may be as justified as any other order, and that it usually comes from a source with superior access to certain information. All cautions considered, it is nonetheless important to study the moral justifications for disobeying an incompetent order. A crisis will leave no time for leisurely deliberation and discussion. Prior ethical analysis and the cultivation of reasoned, principled convictions are therefore essential.

An equally difficult moral problem in the military results from the conflict between a lawful order and a personal moral conviction. For instance, a person believing it wrong to kill innocent people might object to conducting a reconnaissance by fire. Perhaps such a conflict is more apparent than real and can be resolved by agreeing on the need for the reconnaissance and the odds against killing innocents. But if the person remains convinced that he will be killing innocent people, then he must assess the strengths of the moral responsibility to obey a legal order on the one hand and a personal moral belief on the other. In another instance, a person who believes it unfair to treat married and unmarried soldiers differently might encounter a policy directing discriminatory treatment. Failing to get the policy changed, the opponent faces the moral question of whether to obey or disobey. For this person, to obey means to act immorally; to disobey means to act unprofessionally. In cases such as these, a necessary if not a sufficient condition of acting in an ethically responsible way is to reason carefully about the problems and to balance the conflicting considerations fairly, without simply searching for the most expedient or personally advantageous solution.

B. False Reporting

Reporting systems in the military service test the integrity of military leaders in many ways. Like members of other professions, they value the reputation of both individuals and the profession. This concern for image can lead to the suppression of information that threatens to make the organization or certain individuals appear less than competent. Yet, on occasion, suppressed or unjustifiably optimistic reports can adversely affect important decisions being made at the highest level of command. Consider the disadvantage to a truce negotiator acting for his nation if his military chiefs report that their men are only firing when fired upon but the negotiator for the other side has information to the contrary. The credibility of the American negotiator is critical, and accurate reporting is essential to establishing such credibility.

The practice of using the "body count" as a measure of combat effectiveness during the Vietnam War provides an instructive case. Laying aside the important question of what one could reasonably conclude from an exact count of dead bodies on a battlefield, military leaders had to determine the status of the dead, a difficult task inviting speculation. It was sometimes tempting to count any dead Vietnamese as an enemy soldier and to overestimate the number of enemy killed during a night attack by assuming that the enemy could have dragged away their own dead and wounded. If commanders created the impression that body counts were the most important measure of a subordinate's success, or insisted upon higher body counts, the reports were sometimes exaggerated. Since the inflated reports were so favorably received and sometimes demanded, the question of "lying" did not arise.

A plethora of opportunities for false reporting accompanies any bureaucratic structure that relies heavily on statistical data as a measure of success. Reporting AWOL (absent without leave) rates accurately can give a unit "bad numbers" compared to other units. Company commanders may adopt the practice of placing AWOLs on leave rosters after the fact, in order to conceal their actual status. Readiness reports of various sorts are crucial to makers of military policy, yet not every commander is willing to report honestly that his men and equipment may not be "ready" or capable of accomplishing their mission. Maintenance officers are often under extreme pressure to report higher rates than the facts justify.

The relentless demand for outstanding performance, the competitive bid for promotion (the individual's strongest measure of success), the fear of seeing a mistake converted to a disaster, disproportionate reliance on quantitative measures of leadership ability—these are some of the pressures that lead to false reporting. Simple as it may seem, perhaps the beginning step in addressing this ethical issue is to recognize and label a false report as a *lie*. The recruiting scandals of the last part of the 1970s present a tragic example of moral myopia in this regard. Hundreds of military recruiters were ultimately disgraced when it was revealed that they loaded computers with names of fictitious recruits, concealed police records of prospective recruits, changed test scores and physical examination records, ignored evidence of past drug usage—all to meet or exceed enlistment quotas. When the recruiters who participated in these dishonest acts were asked by Congressional committees why they did not point out to superiors that the quotas were too high, one person said, "When you're given a mission, you don't question the mission." Another response was, "My superiors knew what we were doing and condoned it." Somehow the notion that an immoral means, lying, was being employed to "accomplish the mission" either did not occur to the dishonest recruiters or, if it did, was easily overcome by the possible knowledge that others higher in the chain of command were aware of the lying practices and had not condemned them.

Examination of false reporting in the military can usefully proceed along two paths: an inquiry into the moral justification of asking for and using reports from subordinates, and a consideration of the conflict between integrity and the hope for promotion. An effective military ethics program would make all military leaders conscious of the serious moral implications of a "statistics mentality" and of false reporting.

C. Careerism

The totally self-seeking person—recognized by many moral philosophers as being outside the pale of moral influence—is usually the first to embrace moral rhetoric and call for the support of moral principles. To live in a society of selfless moral paragons is to enjoy the best chance for promoting one's own selfish ends and "getting over" those trusting souls who treat others fairly. Thus, in military service, the careerist, the person intent only on advancing to the best jobs and the highest rank, no matter what the cost to other people or to the service, is likely to be a person professing concern about ethics in the military. A careerist rarely claims to be one. In combating careerism, therefore, military leaders often seize upon any hint that a person is interested in his own well-being as sure evidence of careerism. Yet people would agree that military leaders naturally want promotion and recognition for services rendered; merely seeking a successful professional life is not unethical in and of itself. The moral issue is not whether totally self-seeking careerism is good—it's not—or whether desire for a successful career is bad—it's not. Instead the ethical problem lies in rationally and rightfully answering the opposing claims of profession and self. These are the conflicts that trouble moral men and women in the military.

As with most moral questions, accurate identification and interpretation of the facts are critical to an enlightened resolution. The facts, hard to ascertain even when one is trying to choose the right action for oneself, are harder to discover about other people. Most talk about careerism centers, however, on the alleged careerism of other people. It is often easier to censure others for self-seeking motives than to identify similar motives in oneself. If leaders confine themselves to the things they know, careerism may become a less pervasive moral problem than they previously believed. Whatever their conclusion, the more they know about the facts in any moral predicament, the better they should be able to analyze it rationally.

That so many officers believe careerism to be a problem in military service suggests an agreement on the facts. More important, the popularity of the belief also suggests a sharing of a similar moral angle for viewing the facts. A different moral angle of vision might possibly lead to a different moral conclusion. Since analysis of facts proceeds from a moral viewpoint, agreement on the facts will not necessarily produce consensus on the morally right action. One person's careerism could be another's self-realization; one person's professionalism, another's insensitive consequentialism. Careful thinking about various moral viewpoints leads one to conclude that the values each person finds in the service, although they may evoke similar judgments from large numbers of military persons, must themselves be fully explained and rationally defended. Agreeing with the majority on moral judgments, even if the majority consists of upstanding military colleagues, does not insure that a military leader has adopted the best moral stance.

On the other hand, the moral beliefs held by American military leaders, as a group, are so universally accepted that any leader who breaks with the majority to promote his self-interest must make an exceedingly strong case for his actions; and usually he cannot do so. The rationalization for self-serving actions tends to be most convincing to people with high estimates of their own worth. For instance, an infantry captain who believes that he will be a better battalion S-3 than any major in the division may make himself morally comfortable with actions designed to draw favorable attention to his accomplishments—even if they entail driving his soldiers into the ground in the pursuit of overly ambitious goals. Or a naval officer might say: "I'll stretch the truth about my qualifications. No one will ever check the record, and I alone deserve command of that ship." Sound moral reasoning rejects those attempts to justify unethical acts, even in the unlikely case that the self-valuation is correct.

The opposite extreme to careerism has no name. By analogy one would call it "professionalism" were the term not already used to mean something highly admirable. Even without a name, however, behavior so "selfless" that it promotes the profession by immoral acts does not become morally right simply because it is "selfless." Stealing a senator's papers critical of an Air Force construction program so as to protect the image of the military profession is as wrong as the most blatant careerism. When professional dedication to service becomes a blind loyalty or a mindless commitment, just as when self-interest becomes a selfish disregard for others, the situation is morally perilous.

D. Efficiency Reports

Evaluating another person's performance of work is a terrible responsibility. Everyone in the military knows that performance reports determine chances for promotion, selection for schooling, and assignment to desirable positions, as well as the likelihood of retention or separation. The potential moral problem, one involving truth-telling and its absence, manifests itself when raters gild the lily or call a thorn a rose. The military seems to worry more about the gilding.

Despite the strictures of the senior-subordinate relationship, senior leaders tend to grow fond of their subordinates and develop toward them a special sense of loyalty and paternalistic concern. Understandably enough, a senior often does not want to harm the prospects for a subordinate whose competent performance offers hope for continued good service. Unfortunately, though, in any competitive rating system restrained praise tends to be interpreted as implied criticism. The logic of the system constantly ups the rating ante. Some people argue that the only way to control the inflation of praise is to nip constantly at the heels of raters. Thus, the services redesign rating forms periodically and introduce a new form when the current one begins to elicit particularly inflated reports. The forms try to force raters to render judgments about the relative worth of good persons. Raters resist those attempts and try desperately to keep all good men in the same category of goodness. Suspicious of other raters and the entire evaluation system, raters want to prevent unfair and unjust treatment of the good persons they rate. If gilding the lily is a moral problem, these raters would say, its nature lies in a decision not to gild and, therefore, to moderate the enthusiasm and optimism stemming from a competent performance. It may be that "damning by faint praise" has a greater claim for moral attention than "complicating by excessive praise." Enthusiastic reports, to be sure, complicate the act of discriminating among good people. But unless military leaders can convince themselves that it is wrong to be generous to a good person, then they should not automatically call extra-glowing reports a moral problem.

A more common moral problem is raised by the enthusiastic

report on a person whose performance has actually been inadequate or whose traits of character seem to be inimical to the successful completion of military missions. Even though he knows that the person lacks the qualities needed in the military profession, the rater sometimes sees strong humanitarian reasons for not being "brutally" truthful: fear that an honest report will have grievous consequences in the person's family; belief that he has no right to cause another person unhappiness; reluctance to say that another person is bad or will not later change for the better. Other restraints may be more common and less noble: avoidance of confrontations; fear of revenge; preference never to give a low report since poor ratings may reflect upon the competence of the superior as well as the subordinate. In the face of such reservations, the rater would be trying to find some kind of justification for his patently immoral act—lying. The deliberation is complicated because raters know that in their reports on good performers with high potential they are not "brutally" truthful, but rather fervidly supportive. If optimism can mark ratings of good performers, why should a rater not be optimistic about poor performers? Does he not lie as much in gilding the lily as in calling a thorn a rose? Dishonesty in the efficiency rating system is thus an extraordinarily pernicious but subtle problem. Hard to define, easy to rationalize, dishonest reports not only produce inefficient operations, they corrupt the moral sensibilities of individuals as well.

E. Protecting the Innocent in War

The soldier, be he friend or foe, is charged with the protection of the weak and unarmed. It is the very essence and reason for his being. When he violates this sacred trust, he not only profanes his entire cult but threatens the fabric of international society.[22]

Commitment to the military profession carries with it a prima facie acceptance of the use of war as an instrument of national policy. Military professionals cannot consistently be pacifists in the normal sense of the term. That acceptance is not, however, a blanket abdication of moral reasoning on the part of military professionals regarding the morality of a specific war, nor does it provide a *carte blanche* regarding the means employed in waging war. When General MacArthur approved Admiral Yamashita's execution after World War II, he affirmed the principle that commanders are responsible for the conduct of their subordinates, even in the most confused and chaotic circumstances. Yamashita did not control his men (and probably he could not have done so) who committed atrocities against civilians and prisoners in the Philippines; he was convicted, although it was never established that he had knowingly ordered any of the atrocities that were committed by his men.

Some moral philosophers (notably Elizabeth Anscombe and John C. Ford) maintain that there are always innocent noncombatants in war and that their natural right to life is intrinsic; i.e., it is always morally wrong intentionally to take the life of the innocent. Thus Ford, arguing not as a pacifist but from the moral tradition of the rules of war, condemned the obliteration bombing of civilian population centers in World War II.[23] Within this tradition a central problem is that of distinguishing combatants from noncombatants and establishing the criteria of "innocence." Recently, Jeffrie Murphy, Thomas Nagel, Richard Brandt, and others have made thoughtful and important attempts at clarifying and resolving this problem.[24] Murphy and Nagel, for example, agree that combatants in war (legitimate enemy targets) are those who pose an immediate threat ("are engaged in an attempt to destroy you"). They distinguish those who support the soldier as a human being (the farmer who provides his food) from those who support him *qua* soldier (manufacturers of munitions). The former are exempt from attack as noncombatants; the latter are not exempt from attack. In addition, Telford Taylor, among others, has attempted to clarify the notion of a "war crime" based on the "laws of war."[25] These are difficult and controversial issues, fraught with ambiguity, but they are issues that military leaders must learn to analyze in conceptually rigorous ways.

Must each military member become an expert on just war theory, the laws of war, and the moral considerations necessary to determine who is "innocent" in war? Certainly every military leader should have done some serious reading and reflecting on the morality of war itself and, even more important, should accept responsibility for observing the laws of war and their attendant moral justifications. If the revelations about My Lai are accurate (unarmed prisoners of all ages and sex were executed by their captors), there can be no excusing the commanding officer on the scene from the charge of issuing both illegal and immoral orders. The cover-up of the My Lai incident by other military leaders was also inexcusable. The My Lai trial received great publicity and much attention, but it was not the first or only such case; many military men were tried and convicted by American military courts in Vietnam and in other wars dating back to the American Civil War for violating the "laws of war and humanity." The instruction that must be given to all military members concerning the rights of noncombatants can never be sufficient to obviate the necessity for individual judgment in specific and ambiguous combat circumstances. Evoking clear thoughts about innocents in war before the fighting begins should sharpen the eventual judgments of military leaders in war.

F. Nuclear, Chemical, and Biological Warfare

The moral issues attendant upon the possible uses of nuclear, chemical, and biological weapons are more frequently discussed by civilian philosophers and theologians than by military writers. Nevertheless, they are real issues in the minds of many morally sensitive military professionals, and they do not admit to simple resolution. Some military officers have avoided or declined duty with the Strategic Air Command's missile wings precisely because they wished to avoid the possibility of having to launch a nuclear warhead. The decision to use nuclear weapons is considered so grave that only the President of the United States may authorize their use by the United States military. President Truman made the difficult decision to drop the atomic bombs in Japan in 1945; and he apparently did so on utilitarian grounds, arguing that it would shorten the war and save more lives in the long run. The problem, however, is to decide when this sort of utilitarianism is appropriate. Those thinkers, such as Ford and Anscombe, who argue on nonutilitarian grounds against intentional attacks on the innocent conclude that Truman's decision was morally incorrect. Some moral philosophers have argued that the vast destructive characteristics of nuclear weapons, including radioactive fallout, make their use impossible without the destruction of enormous numbers of noncombatants and hence make modern war itself immoral. Others maintain that under certain conditions, just wars may still be fought employing nuclear weapons aimed at counterforce targets. Gregory Kavka has written a thought-provoking analysis of the moral issues involved in using the threat of nuclear weapons to deter future attacks.[26] He argues that the intention to retaliate against a possible nuclear attack may play an important role in deterring the attack. But if the intention is to retaliate by destroying the attacker's civilian population centers, then we risk violating a classical moral bridge principle, namely, "To intend to do what one knows to be wrong is itself wrong." As Kavka explores further "paradoxes" of deterrence, he concludes that there is an "apparent incompatibility of the moral principles we use to evaluate acts and agents."

Clearly the issue of nuclear weapons is profoundly difficult, and the deterrence argument may require, as Kavka suggests, a complete rethinking of our ways of evaluating agents and actions. The military uses of chemical and biological weapons pose similarly complex and troublesome issues. Richard Krickus suggests that if we separate biological from chemical considerations, it is possible to show that biological weapons cannot be classified under classical just war theory because they cannot be sufficiently controlled.[27] He argues, however, that chemical weapons, especially nonlethal types that might temporarily incapacitate people, "might well fit within the parameters of the just war doctrine." Indeed, he suggests that such chemical weapons may possibly make the waging of limited warfare more humane.

Given the importance of nuclear deterrence in the international environment and continuing press reports on the development of chemical and biological weapons in various countries, military leaders must not avoid thinking about the ethical issues involved in their use. Nothing could be more undesirable and in the long run more dangerous, than for military scholars to concentrate exclusively on the strategic or technical aspects of these issues, leaving the ethical questions to civilian philosophers or theologians. If the moral dimensions of these matters are to receive the urgent attention they deserve in our society, ethical analysis must come from within the military profession as well as from outside it.

In addition to the six issues discussed here, the military profession faces many other moral problems that become distinctive in a military context. The conduct of military operations against a hostile force raises, for example, questions about military necessity, limitations on the use of force, and actions against terrorists and guerrillas. Preparation for war raises questions about realism and risk in training, the recruitment of a fighting force, and the assignment of people in the military service. In all probability, some of the military's most acute moral problems are those it has not yet fully recognized. It is to be hoped, therefore, that the careful study of a wide variety of the military's known ethical issues will develop in students the ability and disposition to detect and think through other moral problems of significance to the profession of arms.

V. Goals in the Teaching of Military Ethics

The purpose of developing a course in ethics, or a more ambitious program, may seem self-evident. Military leaders ought to be moral people, and the purpose of ethics teaching should be the promotion of that ideal. But a general statement of that kind is ultimately not very illuminating. In fact, there are a number of different possible goals for the teaching of ethics: to improve character, to change behavior, to develop sensitivities, to foster intellectual and practical skills, to indoctrinate particular values, to understand moral traditions, and so on. All of these goals can be perfectly valid and acceptable. But it is not necessarily possible to achieve, or even sensibly aim for all of these goals at the same time, especially in the classroom. Priorities may have to be set, and some goals emphasized more than others.

It is critical that courses or programs in ethics have clear goals and purposes, and that these be understood by the students in the courses, by those assigned to teach them, and by those in higher authority who are ultimately responsible for them. A failure to be clear about goals can lead to misunderstanding, false expectations, unrealistic modes of evaluation, and, ultimately, general disillusionment that the venture has any value at all. No course or program in ethics is likely to change an inveterate scoundrel into a paragon of virtue, nor can programs in ethics be guaranteed to change ordinary behavior and produce morally exemplary armed forces. To expect such outcomes is to ignore some important realities: moral attitudes and behavior are influenced by family background and the general culture of a society, by the implicit moral messages often conveyed by institutional arrangements, by the different circumstances of individual lives and professional tasks. Taken together, those influences can far more decisively alter attitudes and behavior than courses in ethics.

What, then, are reasonable goals in the teaching of ethics? In general, a well-designed and well-taught program should provide a decent introduction to the military profession, to its major value characteristics, and to its basic rules and responsibilities. It ought also to convey a point of fundamental importance: ethical behavior is not something merely desirable to add to other professional skills, it is an integral part of deploying those skills and using them most effectively.

The ultimate moral purpose of the military profession is that of protecting and defending the nation and its deepest values. That higher moral purpose cannot be divorced from the means chosen to pursue it. Generally speaking, a course, even a very short one, can make clear that ethical thinking and analysis require the same degree of rigor as do other subjects, that the field of ethics is one of long-standing and careful human thought, and that no single course can pretend to do adequate justice to the problems. A serious course in ethics must, then, be something more than an occasion for moral exhortation, the telling of war stories, and the purveying of personal opinions and observations.

More specifically, what are other reasonable goals?

1. Stimulating the Moral Imagination

It can never automatically be assumed that everyone is aware of the existence of moral problems, or the full range of those problems. The way individuals and organizations behave can and often will affect the lives of others; our actions have consequences for human welfare. Sensitivity about those consequences for the lives of those who will be affected by our actions requires imagination and insight. Moreover, a course in ethics ought not be an abstract exercise of logic—empathy, feeling, and caring are emotional traits that are imperative if one is to understand the moral life and moral relationships among people and nations.

Human beings make mistakes, they can often act stupidly or irrationally, they often fail to live up to their own ideals, and they are sometimes grossly hypocritical. Moral ideals are not easy to achieve, and life has a way, whether in war or peace, of confounding our hopes, plans, and ideals. Morality cannot be understood fully or with sensitivity unless those human realities are explored and carefully considered.

2. Recognizing Moral Issues

A stimulation of the moral imagination ought quickly to be joined to a careful effort to identify and describe moral problems. While the realm of morality overlaps in many places with that of politics or law or military leadership, the chief characteristic of an ethical issue is that it raises basic questions of rights and obligations, of good and evil, of the ends and purposes of individual lives and those of major social institutions. A basic reason for the difficulty of ethics, and for the disagreement it can engender, is the profundity of its questions and the enormous implications of the answers achieved. A course in ethics should lay out the major moral questions that face those in the military, show why they make a difference, and show the possible consequences, for good or bad, of different answers. In some cases, good moral conduct will turn on adherence to an accepted moral rule or principle. In other cases, rules or principles may not be clear, or are too general to be of help in resolving specific cases. At that point, the wise exercise of personal and professional virtue, and of reflective prudence, may be the key requirement.

3. Developing Analytical Skills

Many moral issues will turn on the way in which we understand some very general concepts, ideas, or virtues. The meaning of terms such as "duty," courage," "integrity," are not instantly clear. They have to be carefully analyzed, and an attempt must be made to distinguish between legitimate and illegitimate uses, richer and thinner meanings. What follows from a commitment to "duty"—that duty toward country always overrides duty to parents or families or friends or subordinates? That lying in the name of "duty" is acceptable? Those can be difficult questions to answer on occasion. A class in ethics ought to provide a significant occasion to grapple with some of them.

Morality in general, and specific moral rules and principles, are subject to better and worse ways of reasoning. What are the implications of following particular moral rules, both in the short and in the long run? A common problem in morality—the classic moral dilemma—is that of trying to weigh and balance different moral rules, both of which ought to be observed. If one ought both to tell the truth and to be responsible for the welfare of one's subordinates, what should be done when only the telling of a lie would seem to promote that welfare? Courses in ethics should provide some guidance in wrestling with dilemmas of that kind. The rational ability to sort out and identify the moral principles or virtues at stake in a decision, and the capacity to analyze them to determine their meanings and implications, may not, in the end, always produce a clear and obvious answer. But that skill can be enormously helpful in getting the problem straight, in possibly eliminating some wrong or harmful answers, and in facilitating more rational discussion. At the least, courses in ethics ought to promote efforts at consistency and coherence in ethical discourse and debate.

4. Eliciting a Sense of Moral Obligation and Personal Responsibility

At the heart of morality is the responsibility of the individual for his or her behavior. A course in ethics should explore the question of moral obligation, of our duty toward others and toward our country. The law, civilian and military, both requires some actions and forbids others and ordinarily backs its statutes with specific penalties for noncompliance. Morality, by contrast, places the heaviest weight of compliance upon the individual in the privacy of his or her conscience; its sanctions include the pain of recognizing that one has violated that conscience or compromised one's integrity and sense of honor.

Military leaders, like all people, have the ordinary range of moral duties: toward their families, their spouses, their children, and their friends. They also have some additional, and in many ways unique, obligations: toward the security of their nation, toward those in their command, and toward their superior officers. A moral life that consists in mere obedience to the law, or to orders, out of fear of punishment hardly deserves the name "moral." The larger question is that of personal obligations—the way in which ethical demands are conscientiously pondered and acted upon, and the development of a life animated by those personal and professional character traits that do honor both to one's person and to one's country. An attempt to understand those demands and virtues, and what they require of us, is central to the work of ethics.

5. Tolerating—and Resisting—Disagreement and Ambiguity

Some moral problems are, in principle, easy to resolve: we know what we ought to do and all that is required is the will and courage to do it—do we have the guts to do what we know (and everyone knows) to be right? Other problems are not easy, either because important duties or rights seem to be in conflict, or because there are reasonable differences of judgment on the right thing to do. These latter problems can make ethics an exceedingly difficult subject, open to considerable ambiguity and sharp disagreements. The ability, up to a point, to tolerate those disagreements and ambiguities is essential. On some occasions, our conscience will be torn and no clear answer will appear; the good we will try to do may cause some evil or harm as well. Often there is simply no escape from that outcome.

At the same time, it is a mistake to accept passively all disagreement and ambiguity. Every effort should be made for greater clarity and for resolution of disagreements as far as possible. Do our moral principles actually require this or that particular action? Have some relevant facts been overlooked that might make a difference in a moral assessment of a situation? Can some practical steps be taken to avoid a moral problem in the first place, or limit its difficulties? Asking questions of that kind can frequently reduce uncertainty or resolve moral debates.

Those five specific goals for the teaching of military ethics need to be placed in context. An implicit assumption behind them is that a course or program on ethics ought strongly to be oriented toward analysis and understanding, and toward a development of the knowledge, skills, and insight necessary to grasp moral problems and to handle them in a thoughtful and rational way.

But will that approach change or influence behavior and will it necessarily lead to better armed forces? That obvious question will bear upon the way courses and programs in ethics ought to be evaluated. Our own belief is that formal courses or programs in ethics should take as their primary task the responsibility of laying a good foundation for ethical behavior in the future. That is best done in the *classroom* by an emphasis on careful reflection, understanding, and analysis. While more effective systems of reward and punishment in the field may improve behavior, and while reiterated moral exhortation in the same context may help as well, the task of a formal course is the rational illumination of the subject matter of ethics. A course in ethics that, say, simply stresses the penalties for violating military law, or consists only in moral exhortation will not deepen understanding or lead to more reflective conduct.

We stress what we believe ought to be sought *"in the classroom"* for a number of reasons. First, it is the general obligation of all leaders to support and promote good moral behavior. That is not a task to be left solely to a course in ethics, which will have limited time and which will, in any case, hardly be able to provide an instant corrective to those situations outside of the classroom that undermine moral behavior. Second, much actual moral behavior will be influenced by the role model provided by those in command. If they fail to provide exemplary moral leadership, no course in ethics can be expected to overcome the power of their bad example. Worse still, a failure of moral leadership at the command level can and often does introduce a moral cynicism that no class in ethics can possibly surmount. Morality, in short, is conveyed in many ways, most of them outside the classroom. Organizational structures, for example, can often create ethical problems that nothing done in a classroom can overcome. Such matters are outside of the control of the instructors and students alike.

For all these reasons, to expect a class on ethics to decisively shape future behavior would be naive. What a course can do is to provide one of the few occasions for formally and systematically examining and discussing matters of morality. In itself, there is no guarantee it will make any difference in behavior. But we do not believe behavior can be effectively influenced without some period of time given to asking, in a serious, systematic, and sustained way, just what morality requires for those in the armed forces. A course can provide the occasion to step back from immediate moral or leadership obligations in order to ask what they mean, to consider what can be done in cases of moral conflict or uncertainty, to provide some solid content to what otherwise might be dismissed as mere hortatory slogans, e.g., "duty, honor, country."

There are some critics who contend that a course in ethics can or will cripple a military leader's ability to make rapid and firm decisions. A leader given to excessive worry and doubt about moral decisions, it has been said, will be unable to command effectively. We see no solid evidence to support that judgment, either in the military or any other profession. On the contrary, since moral problems will *inevitably* be encountered in the military, as in any other profession, it would be short-sighted as well as irresponsible to deny military leaders an occasion to think about them, to anticipate them, and to find help in deciding what can be done about them. Sound judgment is no less important than decisiveness. Finally, a course in ethics should induce a careful assessment of the moral justification for the accepted standards and values of the profession. If that justification is not understood, critically appraised, and accepted personally, then the moral foundations will simply not exist for the total dedication required of a member of the armed forces.

VI. Evaluation of Ethics Teaching

After Watergate, William Sloan Coffin wrote a poignant essay in the *New York Times* (June 19, 1973, p. 39) recalling that he had been Jeb Magruder's ethics teacher at Williams College. "Teaching is at best a precarious business," observed Coffin. "The rational mind is no match for an irrational will that needs to place popularity and power above truth."

Coffin's reflection on the relationship between his teaching and Magruder's behavior fourteen years later raises questions that deserve special attention in a military context. Since American military forces exist only to fulfill an explicit constitutionally mandated purpose, any missions they undertake must be assessed in light of this purpose. In the teaching of ethics, therefore, military teachers must have clearly articulated goals. Such teachers must also expect to have their performance, and the whole enterprise of teaching ethics, evaluated in light of these goals. They should want to know if they are achieving their own objectives, and if overall the program is achieving its goals. Just as the military's failing to fulfill its constitutional purpose should lead to the replacement of commanders who trained and directed the force, so a failed ethics program should lead to the dismissal of teachers who shaped and directed the program.

But it is easier to determine that a war is lost than that the armed forces are not morally developed. If one in a thousand students acts immorally, even if his action be as nationally significant as Magruder's, has that student's teacher failed to meet his goal? Has the program itself failed? Does taking responsibility for

51

teaching ethics mean taking responsibility for a student's subsequent behavior, even years after the course? And if program and teacher are not responsible for students who eventually act immorally or give evidence of moral blindness or ignorance, can program and teacher take any credit for a student's demonstrations of moral virtue?

Some people might be inclined to argue against any measurement of how well students meet the teaching objectives of classes in the humanities. If one identifies and accepts a set of goals, however, then the very meaning of "goals" calls for a measure of achievement. For the teaching of ethics in the military, the issue is not whether achievement should be measured, but, rather, what counts as achievement, what method best measures it, and what boundaries constitute the proper limits to the measurements.

One widely followed approach uses a scale of moral judgment and measures students on the scale according to their responses to hypothetical moral dilemmas. A popular model, propounded by Lawrence Kohlberg, divides moral judgments into six categories or stages, each allegedly more moral than the one before. Controversial though these categories may be, they offer a handy measurement of moral development. If through discussion and testing a teacher could place a new student at a stage-three level of moral development, for instance, then, if the student has advanced to stage four by the end of the course, perhaps he should count his course a success. Stipulating moral categories, however, promises more than it delivers. The classification achieved in the classroom is at best merely a predictor—maybe right, maybe wrong—of daily behavior in the workaday world. It seems to offer little more insight to out-of-class behavior than more conventional methods of measurement such as written essays or oral examinations. (For an analysis of conventional or traditional approaches to the evaluation of the teaching of ethics see Arthur L. Caplan, "Evaluation and the Teaching of Ethics," in *Ethics Teaching in Higher Education*, eds. D. Callahan and S. Bok (New York: Plenum Press, 1980), pp. 133–50.)

Conventional methods also use categories in calling for an exhibition of moral reasoning: evidence showing mastery of all course goals merits an "A"; less persuasive evidence, a "B"; and so on. Conventional testing gives a sound index of how well a student has intellectually achieved the goals specified in Part V. Well-structured essay questions in particular give students the chance to demonstrate their moral imagination, their ability to recognize moral issues, their analytical skill, their mastery of the arguments for being moral, and their facility to deal on paper with contentious and ambiguous issues. We cannot recommend too strongly the careful reading of essays written by students as the best way to evaluate how well they have met course objectives. Moreover, the record of their thinking serves as a splendid foundation for productive conferences between student and teacher.

Evaluation of how a person thinks in the classroom seems to be insufficient for many leaders in the military, however. Commanders want people to do the right thing, not merely to show a facility for discussing the right behavior. The behavioral measure has strong appeal in a profession that customarily measures itself by results. For years military leaders have looked for indications of unit morale (and, for some people, morality) in the statistics reflecting AWOL rates, criminal activity, VD cases, and the like. On efficiency reports, raters often must comment on the professional ethics of the person being rated. Employing statistics and rating behavior, the military would seem interested, not in the goals outlined in Part V, but simply in whether someone is doing what leaders think should be done.

There is no empirical data establishing that the person who masters the objectives set forth for the teaching of ethics will, in fact, act in a morally responsible way in his profession; the best student may not have the will to act on personal knowledge. Likewise, there is no empirical data establishing that persons who act in a morally responsible way in their profession actually met the stated goals of instruction in the ethics classroom; the class dunce may be the person of strongest moral character. Thus, measuring a person's overt behavior in his profession as an index of how well the teacher has met his avowed classroom objectives makes no sense. That is also why simply "acting right" is not one of the objectives of teaching ethics to military leaders. Hopes for education in ethics have logical limits.

Discussion of evaluation methods, perhaps more than any other subject, helps one realize how much the teaching of ethics trades on hope. Leaders hope that morally aware and knowledgeable students will act in a morally reasonable fashion, not just at the end of the course but every day of their lives. Leaders hope that sound moral convictions courageously voiced in class will turn into courageous action on other fields on other days. When students-turned-graduates fail to fulfill the profession's hopes, however, the response should not be automatically to fault the teachers or the endeavor of teaching ethics. Hopes entail no responsibilities. The ultimate responsibility to perform lies with the student, not the leader.

It is understandable, nevertheless, that the military should want to know if a course has met its objectives and won the confidence of its students. The essay examination is only one measure of that knowledge. Quality of discussion in class and ability to answer objective questions provide other indicators. The case study—an actual or hypothetical situation constituting a complete, fully described world in and of itself—is an excellent basis for writing or discussion. It also forces the teacher to come to terms with his own moral reasoning since he is obliged to show his own power of analysis in discussing the particulars of the case.

Surveys measuring the attitudes of students toward the course and the teacher are of special merit. If a survey merely aims at discovering whether "values" have changed, as indicated by answers given on the first and last day of classes, for example, one should note that "changing values" is not an objective. While a student's values may change—"temperance" may fall a notch below "generosity"—the functional worth of such data appears dubious. Of more significance would be students' testimony, sometime after the course, about moral problems that they have recognized and dealt with in an intellectually sound way. Also of interest would be revelations that their studies actually hampered their ability to reason morally, or that their teachers had somehow destroyed a desire to discover and do what a person ought to do.

Concerned as leaders should be about the positive effect of teaching ethics in the military, they should remember that the most precarious element in their endeavor is close to home: namely, the moral reasoning of those who mandate educational programs, to say nothing of the teachers themselves. Though we cannot present it as a fact, we have observed that military leaders tend to discuss privately the ethics of their superiors and publicly the ethics of their subordinates. Many leaders seem to care more about what other people should do than about what they themselves should do. Since only we can make ourselves find the right and do the right, a military leader's primary subject in evaluation should be himself. If military leaders, particularly at the top, come to think like outstanding students in the ethics classes they have established, then the teaching of ethics will have been successful, with no other evaluation required.

VII. Teaching Techniques and Problems

The teaching of professional ethics in the military cannot be adequately addressed by describing a single academic course that should be taught to all members of the profession. People enter the profession at different levels in the hierarchy and at different ages, with varying intellectual abilities and educational and social backgrounds. The eighteen-year-old enlistee from a broken home who has not completed high school and whose life style has been characterized by ego-centered survival techniques presents one extreme as he attempts to adjust to the professional military ethic. The fifty-year-old general officer with an advanced engineering degree, combat experience in the Vietnam War, a host of subordinates, and the task of preparing them for successful deployment in some future war presents another extreme. The needs at these extremes, and in between, are so clearly different that they point up an obvious fundamental: *what* to teach and *how* to teach it must be determined by *who* is to be taught and *who is available* to do the teaching. At all levels professional ethics must elicit an adherence to the principles of "duty, honor, country" and must find a way of developing moral character that includes the traits of integrity, courage, loyalty, obedience, and subordination of the self to the good of the whole (unit, country). The general should not need to be convinced of the importance of professional ethics, but he may be in need of rationale and renewal. The first-term enlisted person may need to explore and be convinced of the need for professional ethics. The general's need to grasp and grapple with the moral issues attending the use of modern weapons systems may be more pressing and of greater duration and have more far-reaching consequences than the beginning soldier's need. Between these two extremes are the warrant officers, noncommissioned officers, junior officers, and field grade officers. For each of these groups different strategies in teaching military ethics are appropriate.

Because of the differing experiences, maturity, and education of students, the approach to teaching military ethics must be adjusted to the most appropriate level for effectiveness. We will discuss some possibilities for choosing the most appropriate material and pedagogical techniques. However, some material that goes under the rubric of military training involves little need for philosophical analysis and can be used in teaching all military personnel. This material includes "The Code of Conduct for Members of the Armed Forces of the United States," which prescribes behavior as a prisoner of war. The nature of this code is such that any instruction concerning its precepts, while it may involve discussion, must take the form of indoctrination. Much the same is true of the "laws of war." Those that are incorporated into United States laws are among the principles that the military oath of office commits service members to obey and defend. Of course, one must know what those laws are so that the commitment can be informed and conscious. In some ways, instruction in the Code of Conduct and the laws of war resembles instruction for law students in the American Bar Association's Code of Professional Responsibility, which acquaints future lawyers with the provisions so that they may pass related questions on the bar exams and avoid future violations and subsequent punishment. Just as practicing lawyers get additional instruction in the ABA Code through the media, when they see or read about violators being punished, so active military professionals learn about the laws of war when fellow professionals are punished for violations and their cases are publicized. Nonetheless, in every profession including the military, ethics instruction must involve more than code indoctrination. By itself, code indoctrination will not achieve the goals of developing moral reasoning and inculcating critical moral virtues, although it may achieve constraints on behavior through fear of punishment.

Too often the inculcation of the military virtues has been assumed to take place automatically or to have been achieved as a result of exhortation. Experience suggests that such assumptions are no longer justified, if indeed they ever were. Instruction in professional military ethics must include considerable attention to the role these virtues play from both a moral and functional point of view. It is possible to provide a rational justification for holding loyalty, courage, and integrity to be important attributes of a person of good moral character on Aristotelian, Kantian, or rule utilitarian grounds. The framework for each of these basic ethical theories can provide us with good reasons for holding that loyalty is better than disloyalty, courage is better than cowardice, and integrity is better than a lack of integrity. Disagreement may arise in application to specific cases (Loyalty to whom? Is *this* the courageous path? Is *that* the most truthful response?); but the status of loyalty, courage, and integrity as important moral virtues is well established.

On the other hand, obedience and selflessness are more in need of justification than the previously mentioned virtues. Most Western moral philosophies have generally insisted upon moral autonomy—one gets little *moral* credit for acting under orders or under coercion of some other sort. Obedience seems virtuous only in some well-established societal hierarchy: children to parents, students to teachers, worker to manager, soldier to officer. In each case the "obligation" to be obedient rests upon either a presumed natural order (child-parent) or contractual agreement. In these contexts the ultimate end is the achievement of order rather than chaos for each social unit. Within the military hierarchy, obedience is justified on two major grounds. First, taking an oath of office to obey all lawful orders, a member of the military grounds the obligation to obey in a formal promise. The second justification rests on pragmatic or utilitarian grounds: without obedience in the military's hierarchial structure, the military function cannot be performed. Similarly, when one takes the oath of office for national military service, one places the good of country above self and, implicitly at least, pledges to risk one's own life in defense of the country. Self-subordination is critical both to the hierarchical military structure and to fighting battles—without it no service person would enter a battle where there is personal risk.

Integrity, courage, loyalty, obedience, selflessness—these are some of the critical moral virtues essential to the military profession. They are virtues in other human endeavors as well; and some, at least, are justified on other than utilitarian grounds. It is important to notice that in the military environment these virtues generate both moral and functional imperatives. Their importance and their justification must be emphasized as part of the instruction in military ethics courses at all levels.

While meeting the need to emphasize certain moral virtues to all audiences, teachers of military ethics should organize their classes with their particular audience in mind. For each audience or student group, we will offer suggestions concerning teaching techniques, subject matter, and the qualifications of teachers.

A. Precommissioning Schools

Since officer-leaders provide examples within the profession of ethical conduct and are viewed as "teachers" of military ethics, it seems fitting to teach military ethics to those who are preparing to be officers. Current commissioning sources include the service academies, Reserve Officer Training Corps (ROTC), Officer Training Schools (OTS), and Officer Candidate Schools (OCS). Since OTS and OCS are different service designations for similar schools, references to one of these programs will apply to either. Because the necessary available time, academic environment, and trained instructional staff for a formal, semester-long course in moral philosophy are most likely to be available at the service academies, we will give extensive consideration to ethics instruction at that level. Elements and techniques of instruction may be used selectively as models for ethics programs at other levels.

B. Service Academies

The service academies provide a four-year academic curriculum leading to an undergraduate degree and serve as professional schools for officer training for the various services. Because of their dual purpose (accredited degree plus officer commissioning), these institutions seem ideally organized to teach military ethics: they have faculty members available to teach undergraduate courses who are also themselves military professionals. Nearly all discussions of the qualifications of those persons teaching professional ethics raise one fundamental question: are experienced professionals or philosophy professors best qualified to teach professional ethics? In our view some mix of rigorous philosophical training and professional experience is essential: either philosophers with extended experience in the profession's problems or practicing professionals who have had some formal philosophical training in ethics are the appropriate teachers of such courses. Failing to find this mixed background in a single individual, team-teaching conducted by a philosophy professor and a professional is the next best solution. Fortunately, at least two of the service academies have active duty officers with both operational military experience and an advanced degree in philosophy available to teach courses in military ethics. In the nonacademy training courses, the military officers who serve as instructors should receive as much career development support in the teaching of ethics as possible.

What content should an ethics course at a military academy pursue? Here we come abruptly to the frequently discussed issue of theory versus practice. Should a course at this level concentrate on the specific ethical problems encountered in the military profession, or should it place total emphasis on acquainting students with the classical ethical theories? Our view is that a reasonable balance between theory and practical problems can be achieved in a three-semester-hour course. In seeking the goals specified in Part V, the course should examine the basic ideas of Plato, Aristotle, Kant, Mill, and the other great thinkers who have influenced the moral philosophy that already touches the lives of these students. This is likely to be the only philosophy course most military academy students take, so it should assist them in acquiring skills in analyzing arguments, especially moral arguments. Like other undergraduate students, cadets at the service academies bring many preconceived notions about the source of moral rules to their study of ethics; many espouse a sort of cultural relativism. Relativism in ethics must be examined and contrasted with the moral justifications developed by some of the

great moral philosophers. Ethical egoism and psychological egoism need to be distinguished and examined, especially because of
the concern for careerism in the military profession. Given the
military's insistence on subordination of the self to the good of
the unit or country, egoistic moral theories need careful examination.

The theory portion of such a course must be balanced with
applied ethics, especially applied military ethics. The role that
ethics plays, or should play, in the military profession should be
examined. The moral virtues with special significance for the military must be identified and their functional significance compared
with their normal moral status.

The moral problems associated with waging war should be
given the most careful analysis. For instance, the pacifist position
might be represented through some readings from its most articulate advocates; if possible, convinced pacifists might be invited to
discuss their views in the classroom. Potential officers should not
postpone confronting these problems until they arise in a wartime
context. Further, they must understand the issues involving the
rights of the innocent in war, in order to develop the moral sensitivity needed by leaders in battle, a sensitivity that should have
been present at My Lai.

The formal ethics course at a service academy should place the
institution's honor system within the broader context of theories
of moral character. The perennial danger exists (as with all pre-
scribed ethical codes) that unsophisticated subscribers to an
"honor code" adopt the code in a narrow and legalistic fashion,
accepting it (sometimes out of fear of drastic sanctions) on a sort
of contractual basis, and disregarding it once the apparent con-
tract ends. If such codes cannot stand the test of rational analysis,
or if they cannot find justification in a carefully reasoned ethical
theory, then their precepts and applications must be questioned
and revised. Honor codes are miniature applied ethics systems,
just as any system of professional ethics is an applied branch of
ethics. Neither can exist independently of the broad view of the
moral life for all people from which it must draw its justification.

Our experience in teaching ethics at a service academy suggests that the kind of course just described is better taught to
upperclassmen who are not still staggering from the everyday

worries of the rites of initiation, who have the time for the necessary reading and reflection, and for whom the issues of war and morality are closer and command more emotional involvement. How to place the materials in the course is a continuing concern. Courses that merely survey classical ethical theories and issues do not capture the imagination of many cadets anymore than such surveys attract nonphilosophy majors at civilian institutions. Courses built around case studies command more inherent interest, but they must go on to the hard work of developing the appropriate analytic rigor and understanding of fundamental moral principles and justifications. Perhaps the first essential task is alerting students at the outset of the course that their study will be practical. Cadets become uncomfortable when you ask whether it is morally permissible to kill another human being in war, whether there are some things worth dying for, whether moral rules are relative to a particular society, or whether there are universal moral principles. These seem to be effective kinds of questions with which to begin moral exploration. Some courses have begun effectively with Dostoevski's "Grand Inquisitor" to raise the issues of moral autonomy and the individual's possible rejection of the freedom to make and be responsible for moral decisions. Plato's *Apology* has on occasion provided the trigger needed to interest students in the "examined" life. Beginning with a well-known military episode fraught with moral issues can sometimes be extremely effective; for example, recruiting scandals, cheating incidents at an academy, My Lai, the Lavelle affair. Dealing with a few practical problems can pique interest in exploring the tougher questions of ultimate moral justification. However, it seems best to postpone careful analysis of the larger problems of war and morality to a latter portion of the course, after students have become accustomed to the careful process of moral reasoning and can recognize the difference between a utilitarian and a deontological justification.

The mode of instruction best suited for this subject matter and audience is a combination of lecture and discussion, as long as class size is less than twenty students. The instructor must be a skillful questioner and resist the temptation to lecture for the entire period. Like medical students, cadets are enamored of the power of science and its promise of definitive answers. Their other courses have rooted them in empirical methodologies—they use computers well. Many students are uncomfortable with moral ambiguities and, not unlike the Great Inquisitor's parishioners, would like to be given the "right" answers, the "school solutions." The ability to reason well, to evaluate or tolerate opposing positions, to see that the toughest moral dilemmas are not easily resolved, and to make moral decisions without guaranteed certainty—these are the skills the ethics professor at a military academy must develop in students. It is easy enough to show the importance of loyalty and obedience to the military profession, and to reveal that honesty is morally better than dishonesty. What students need is the ability to judge the honest thing to do in the here-and-now complex case when no ethics teacher is around, or to decide which would be the loyal act and where their highest loyalty lies when there are conflicts. Straight lecturing is not likely to develop these skills in ethics students, nor are batteries of multiple-choice tests. The best teaching environment has teacher and student exploring ethical positions and ethical problems together, with the teacher leading the way but forcing students to *think* rather than *memorize*. Written assignments that require the student to analyze tough ethical issues are helpful; examinations aimed at measuring understanding are better than those merely seeking memorized information.

Military ethics is taught at service academies apart from the formal ethics courses. At some academies all military ethics is taught in military science courses, as part of leadership courses and training, through the chaplains' programs, and through the training developed around the honor system. The importance of loyalty, obedience, integrity, courage, and selflessness can be emphasized in these experiences as well as in military history courses and literature courses. But these programs will probably not enhance moral reasoning or aid in the search for the ultimate foundations or justifications of moral values; nor will they acquaint students with the views of the classic moral philosophers and the complex moral concerns involved in just war issues. At service academies, a formal academic ethics course taught by a military faculty trained in philosophy provides a sound framework that supports and prepares students for instruction in other courses touching on military ethics.

C. ROTC

ROTC students normally are seeking a baccalaureate degree at a civilian university or college. They usually enroll in a military science course each term. The courses are variously designed by the services to acquaint students with subjects such as military tradition and history, the United States defense policy, and basic leadership and tactics. These students could be advised by their ROTC instructors to take a course in ethics from the philosophy department on their respective campuses. Such a course could accomplish several of the goals already mentioned (particularly the introduction of ethical theories and the development of moral reasoning skills) but would not normally focus on the role of ethics in the military profession or morality and war. ROTC instructors could be prepared to offer a course in professional military ethics similar to the one recently designed for that purpose by the Army's Soldier Support Center team at Fort Benjamin Harrison. That course is now being taught to all Army ROTC students and is so completely packaged (with instructor readings, complete lesson plans, a text and supplementary readings for student use, and a design for twelve lecture-discussion sessions) that instructors can prepare easily through a reasonable amount of reading and instructor training workshops. Thus the combination of a standard ethics course taught by civilian philosophy professors and a shorter course on professional military ethics taught by military officers (perhaps with consultation from the philosophy department) could accomplish the several goals of a sound military ethics instruction program.

D. OTS

Students in officer training programs on military bases of the various services may have already earned an undergraduate college degree but have had neither a service academy nor ROTC preparation. The typical OTS or OCS program, aimed at orienting officer candidates to military service, takes approximately three months and includes a vigorous physical military training program. In this environment it does not appear feasible to offer

a semester-long ethics course or to find instructors with philosophical backgrounds to teach such a course. Some hours, of
course, are already devoted to teaching military ethics, generally
through discussions of short articles and case studies. In some
OTS programs the values clarification approach is used in seminar sessions. But case study discussions and values clarification
sessions run the risk of failing to clarify the role of reason in
ethics, thus confirming the views of those who entered the course
with the belief that moral judgments must always be subjective
and relative. In the OTS environment it might be useful to offer a
short course in professional ethics similar to the one described for
Army ROTC students. If instructors could be given materials and
background papers prepared by experienced, professional ethics
teachers, and if they could attend workshops conducted by experienced military teachers of ethics, the result might be a course
that would accomplish the stated goals of military ethics instruction.

E. Military Staff Colleges and War Colleges

The midcareer officers at the staff colleges and the senior
officers at the war colleges pose challenges of a different sort for
military ethics instruction. These experienced professionals have
been involved in the military's moral decisionmaking process for
several years. They have war stories to tell about the unethical or
unprofessional conduct they have witnessed, and their idealism
has often been tempered, if not replaced, by cynicism. Yet in
seminars at their respective professional schools we have found
them to be universally concerned about maintaining or raising the
standards of professional military ethics. However, core instruction specifically directed to military ethics is minimal in most of
these programs. In some, carefully selected speakers have been
effective in generating serious reasoning about the role of ethics
in command decisions; and some seminars have been equally
fruitful.

The question of who should teach ethics at staff colleges and
war colleges poses a problem. The most successful elective ethics
courses have been those taught with the aid of a visiting philoso-

phy professor. But senior officers with scholarly credentials in ethics are few, and philosophy professors with appropriate military experience are scarce. Junior officers, even with the best scholarly credentials, are not likely to hold this group's interest, nor are civilian professors who cannot identify with specific issues in military ethics. Perhaps senior military officers who have completed tours teaching ethics at the service academies would be the best teachers for this audience. In addition, if the few civilian professors who have dealt sufficiently with military issues were to give a lecture series to all students and follow up with small group seminars, sensitivities might be reawakened or reinforced. An elective course aimed at improving moral reasoning and taught by a qualified civilian or senior military instructor can succeed. Presentations from successful military leaders whose high ethical standards are well known and whose ability to articulate the ethical issues is well established can trigger important ethical reflections at staff and war colleges. Of course, the teachers must recognize and meet the need for intellectual rigor at this as at every level of study.

Military professionals at midcareer and those approaching flag rank positions teach professional ethics by the example they provide and the policies they promulgate. They have a special need to acquire sensitivity to institutional programs that may appear to reward unethical conduct. They have the special obligation of pondering the moral complexities involved in the use of modern weapons. At this level teachers must provide the maximum opportunity for discussion led by thoughtful people with appropriate experience. Developing a successful ethics program for the senior service schools is as complex as developing such a program for mature physicians, lawyers, and judges. But the senior service schools are already in existence. The critical challenge is to prepare appropriate instructors and discussion leaders.

F. Training Commands

Professional ethics instruction has a place in basic training and in the technical and branch schools of all the services. In these contexts very little can be done fruitfully with ethical theories at the scholarly level, but much can be done with direct ethical applications. Some existing programs employ case studies extensively and exclusively; others have developed a values clarification approach. Many of these programs are developed and taught by the chaplains assigned to the training commands. Since most of the chaplains have studied moral philosophy or theological ethics, they are possibly prepared to teach ethics, but they must be sensitive to a number of difficulties associated with the training command environment.

There is perennial concern that material taught by chaplains contains implicit, if not explicit, religious proselytizing, so that chaplains teaching ethics must overcome an initial suspicion or overt hostility about the content of their course. Some instruction at the training level must deal with the Code of Conduct and the laws of war and hence appears to be simple indoctrination: instruction seeks to inform and clarify but not necessarily to develop moral reasoning. At this level emphasis can be placed on the critical role of the military virtues and on the traditions of military honor. Both the case studies approach and the values clarification approach have a drawback: they may foster the natural tendency of this audience toward value relativism of the most subjective kind. The instructor needs to generate the attitude that moral reasoning does count, that some ethical arguments are better than others, that some ethical choices can be justified with better reasons than others. If all values receive equal weight, then loyalty, obedience, honesty, courage, and self-subordination lose their special significance for the military function. In evaluating cases, some basic assumptions, for example, "honesty is better than dishonesty," need to be pointed out. The same is true for the process of values clarification: it is insufficient merely to discover what one's values may be; those values must be subjected to close examination with respect to their relationship to the military profession and its societal function.

In basic training and in the technical schools (or branch schools) of the services, ethics instruction can be associated with the general mission of the military profession and with the specific mission of the technical specialties (e.g., honesty in maintaining supply accounts, in the use of government property, in maintenance reports). In basic training, ethics teaching may best be integrated with instruction on the traditions and mission of the profession; in technical schools it can be linked with instruction concerning the technical function under discussion. At the technical and branch school level, assigned instructors can be prepared to teach applied ethics materials. At present, the Army's Soldier Support Center ethics team is developing a short (twelve-lesson) course for use in branch schools. Materials for this course will be so complete that, as in the case of the Army ROTC course, instructors can be ready to use these materials in a short period of time.

G. Warrant Officer and NCO Schools

The variety of schools for warrant officers and noncommissioned officers, which are structured by the services and major commands within the services, provides special opportunities for professional ethics instruction to military leaders who hold crucial positions in the chain of command. It seems feasible that a short course—with supporting materials that highlight specific ethical problems—could be developed for use in these schools. If readings, lesson plans, and instructor guides were developed as thoroughly as those prepared by the staff at the Soldiers Support Center for Army ROTC students and instructors, these schools' regular teaching staffs could, with reasonable effort, teach the professional ethics materials.

Teaching ethics to military people is challenging because of the variety of environments and audiences involved. Service academy and ROTC students present the most traditional audiences for ethics courses, with their collegial context and the availability of specifically educated teachers. They are also one of the most important groups to whom professional military ethics should be taught since they will inherit the responsibilities of moral leadership. Officer Training Schools face a more difficult problem with ethics instruction, for their training period is brief and instructors with adequate ethics backgrounds are scarce. In the professional military education system of the services, we have seen some very decent possibilities for the continuing development of ethics programs at the field grade and senior officers schools. The junior officers schools (for example, the Air Force's Squadron Officers

School) are of short duration, like OTS, but they too could expand their current ethics instruction from a few hours of lecture and discussion to something like the Army ROTC course mentioned earlier. Those officer leaders who receive ethics instruction must themselves assume the responsibility for developing ethics programs in the units they command, at the basic training level, and in the various service technical courses. Officers with strong backgrounds in the study of moral philosophy should be employed as a resource in all of the professional education programs; their ability to provide sound courses in professional ethics should not be restricted to the service academies. A blend of ethical theory with a consideration of practical problems is more easily possible and appropriate in a collegial context; a much greater emphasis on practical problems is appropriate in nonacademic contexts (basic training, unit training). The most difficult (but not insurmountable) problem is to find qualified instructors who will bring substance and innovative techniques to ethics instruction in the variety of learning situations within the military profession. But behind this discussion of possible ways of teaching professional ethics in the military is the assumption that some sort of central direction is needed to guide and encourage teaching at the various levels. Clearly, systematic training programs with consistency, longevity, and appropriate authorization must sustain ethics teaching beyond the immediate interest of the particular teacher or program organizer. The establishment of the special professional ethics staff by the Army at the Soldiers Support Center at Fort Benjamin Harrison, Indiana, and the early products of that staff show promise of providing the continuing central support needed.

Hierarchical bureaucracies tend to respond, however sluggishly at times, to the specific directives of persons at the top, the commanders. If the commander pushes hard for quality in ethics instruction, if he gives it a very high priority, the chances for a healthy program are excellent. The example each commander sets and the standards he demands become his most effective teaching tools.

VIII. Recommendations for the Future

People leading the military today are heirs to an impressive tradition. A modern military leader wanting to be right and wanting his profession to be right does not face the task of reversing a history of indifference to ethical thinking within the profession. On the contrary, American military forces have often distinguished themselves by their extraordinary concern for the moral justification of their actions. The armed forces have cultivated the development of moral virtues. No military leader in the service of the United States can claim that his attention to right and wrong is breaking new ground in the profession.

Yet if today's military leader is advocating the formal teaching of ethics in the profession, he can justifiably think of himself as something of a pioneer. Systematic and ambitious initiatives in teaching during the past few years have had to build on a very narrow base of experience. It is notable, therefore, that so much has happened and that so many programs have been started. Still, the entire venture in the armed forces has the air of an exploratory expedition, even when supported by powerful offices in the hierarchy. Proper behavior is a well-mapped subject for hortatory speeches and articles, but ethics in the military, as an object of systematic, serious, formal study by the profession's leaders, remains mostly undiscovered.

The grass-roots interest in moral reasoning does not have its origin in the appeal of glamorous hardware, exotic TDY trips, or star-garnering assignments. Instead, the interest grows out of a desire by military leaders to develop their capacity for reasoning to a morally sound conclusion. They want to understand their own moral responsibilities, examine their own ethical beliefs in the context of the special demands of military life, and discuss problems of mutual interest with other concerned men and women. They know that military service confronts them with a host of circumstances that do not easily yield firm indications of the morally right action to be performed. Thus, the interest in education in ethics, centering as it does on moral reasoning about problems actually encountered in the armed forces, doubles back on the circumstances out of which the interest comes.

The goals that should guide the military's current and future programs in the teaching of ethics are consistent with the spirit of at least part of the present movement. Although some leaders may want to set grandiose goals and expect from the teaching of ethics a moralistic exhibition—a kind of great ethical awakening marked by dramatically visible conversion—the wisest leaders content themselves with difficult but modest goals that can be reached effectively in the classroom under the direction of a skilled teacher using good teaching material. Hoping and reasonably expecting to see attitudes and actions change in time, leaders and teachers and students should form realistic expectations when they rely on conventional methods of evaluation to determine how well students within the classroom have assimilated the course of instruction. These expectations can account for the unpredictable, individualistic development of moral consciousness and of skill in moral reasoning.

The programs for teaching ethics throughout the military service must, of course, take many forms. The variables that shape a particular curriculum are those affecting any educational program. Because the military academies enjoy the leisure and resources to teach ethics in the most traditional sense, their curricula can reasonably serve as a paradigm for other programs in the military. As the professional experience of students grows, the strategy for achieving the ultimate goals naturally changes. Likewise, as the time available for teaching fluctuates, so too do the enabling objectives of any particular course differ. To be useful, teachers must adjust their programs of instruction to the experience and needs of their students.

Like any other organized program in the military, the teaching of ethics needs the earnest support of commanders if it is to survive and improve. Commanders, however, might well be wary. Few of them have ever studied ethics; the very introduction of the subject might imply to military leaders a questioning of their past judgments. They might also worry about the effectiveness of a military force full of amateur philosophers constantly checking the moral temperature of the environment. Indeed, commanders might harbor all of the objections to the teaching of ethics discussed in Part I. If they understand the counterarguments and recognize the strength of the positive reasons for the enterprise, however, we believe they will know how important the teaching of ethics is to the health of the profession and the country they serve. In short, if commanders understand the intrinsic importance of command support, then they themselves will act in a way consistent with this first recommendation.

Experienced commanders who respond to the call for their support will appreciate the practical motives behind our second recommendation—the armed forces must insure that prospective teachers are educated well, though the demands and thoroughness of the education will severely limit the number of people fully prepared to teach ethics. No profession can, or should, tolerate a bad ethics program. Teachers must know their subject and be able to teach it. They must be recognized military leaders of the highest reputation. They must want to teach ethics because they believe in the power of moral reasoning. They must be willing to act as an energetic nucleus for the activity revolving about them and finding its intellectual source in them. This recommendation borrows from the wisdom of the Marine Corps in declaring for a few good men and women to form the highly skilled center of a program in teaching ethics in the military.

Our third recommendation follows hard on the second. There is a great need for the centralized direction of the development and production of teaching materials, and for the uniform training of teachers who conduct subcourses at various educational levels. Since leaders unschooled in the teaching of ethics will, in fact, be doing most of the teaching, both formal and informal, they must have material that wisely guides their teaching and effectively educates them for their task. The resources listed in Part IX will be of great value, but only centralized direction within each service can produce the specific, detailed, realistic material required by the thousands of leaders in the military. Attractive though the idea of a joint service center for the teaching of ethics may be, centralized control should rest within each service, if for no other reason than the need for communicating directly in the idiosyncratic idiom distinguishing each service.

To prevent possible intellectual isolation within individual services, a fourth course of action recommends itself. The military services should support conferences, workshops, and seminars that bring together people with special interests and roles in the teaching of ethics. Support should continue for the Joint Services Conference on Professional Ethics. Meetings sponsored by training commands should continue. Funds should be regularly available to pay for the attendance of military leaders at civilian assemblies on the teaching of ethics and professional ethics.

As the military acts on the first four recommendations, leaders at all levels must remind themselves of the purpose of their undertaking. The enterprise must not get out of hand. The guidance in Part V of this monograph sets boundaries as well as objectives for the teaching of ethics in the military. Military leaders who want to be right and who want their profession to be right will respect the limitations and take the goals seriously for themselves.

Notes

1. Francis Lieber, 1863, as cited in Telford Taylor, *Nuremberg and Vietnam: An American Tragedy* (New York: Bantam Books, 1971), p. 41.

2. Thucydides, *History of the Peloponnesian War*, Great Books Foundation Edition (Chicago: Henry Regnery Company), pp. 127–30.

3. Telford Taylor, *Nuremberg and Vietnam*, especially pp. 22 ff.

4. Ibid., p. 87.

5. C. Robert Kemble, *The Image of the Army Officer in America* (Westport, Conn.: Greenwood Press, 1973), p. 23.

6. Telford Taylor, *Nuremberg and Vietnam*, see especially chaps. 1 and 4.

7. From a letter "To the President of Congress," September 24, 1776, as quoted in C. Robert Kemble, *The Image of the Army Officer*, p. 17.

8. Alfred Vagts, *A History of Militarism* (New York: Free Press, 1959).

9. Ibid., p. 42.

10. Diane Bornstein, *Mirrors of Courtesy* (Hamden, Conn.: The Shoe String Press, 1975).

11. Ibid., p. 43.

12. Ibid., p. 44

13. Alfred Vagts, *A History of Militarism*, p. 45.

14. C. Robert Kemble, *The Image of the Army Officer*. p. 24.

15. Morris Janowitz, *The Professional Soldier* (New York: The Free Press, 1960 and 1971), p. 215.

16. Ibid., p. 217.

17. Ibid., p. 219.

18. U.S. Department of Defense, Armed Forces Information Service, *The Armed Forces Officer* (1975), p. 3.

19. Morris Janowitz, *The Professional Soldier*, p. 222.

20. *Great Dialogues of Plato*, trans. W.H. Rouse (New York: New American Library, 1956), p. 434.

21. Ibid., p. 456.

22. General Douglas MacArthur made this statement when he confirmed the death penalty for Admiral Yamashita after World War II. Quoted on the frontispiece of Telford Taylor's *Nuremberg and Vietnam: An American Tragedy*.

23. John C. Ford, S. J., "The Morality of Obliteration Bombing," *Theological Studies* 5 (1944): 261–309; reprinted in abridged form in Richard A. Wasserstrom, *War and Morality* (Belmont, Calif.: Wadsworth Publishing Co., 1970).

24. Jeffrie G. Murphy, "The Killing of the Innocent," *The Monist* 57, no. 4 (1973); Thomas Nagel, "War and Massacre," *Philosophy and Public Affairs* 1, no. 2 (1972); Richard B. Brandt, "Utilitarianism and the Rules of War," *Philosophy and Public Affairs* 1, no. 2 (1972). Reprinted in Malham M. Wakin, *War, Morality, and the Military Profession* (Boulder, Colo.: Westview Press, 1979).

25. Telford Taylor, *Nuremberg and Vietnam*, especially chaps. 1 and 2.

26. Gregory Kavka, "Some Paradoxes of Deterrence," *The Journal of Philosophy* 75 (June, 1978); reprinted in Malham M. Wakin, *War, Morality, and the Military Profession*.

27. Richard J. Krickus, "On the Morality of Chemical/Biological War," *Journal of Conflict Resolution* 9 (June 1965); reprinted in Malham M. Wakin, *War, Morality, and the Military Profession*.

IX. Bibliographical Sources

This section is intended to serve those interested in substantive materials on military ethics, particularly those who are seeking materials suitable for teaching military ethics. Materials are categorized for practical usefulness. No attempt has been made to be complete, and single articles have not been listed (many are contained in the anthologies). The sources listed here will provide good leads and suggestions for further material.

A. Ethics and the Military Profession

1. *American Behavioral Scientist*, May/June, 1976, volume 19, no. 6, Sage Publications, Beverly Hills, Calif. 90212. This entire issue, edited by Sam C. Sarkesian and Thomas M. Gannon, is devoted to military ethics and professionalism. Some of the articles are anthologized elsewhere. Several of them are suitable for use in military ethics courses with assigned readings.

2. Brown, James and Michael J. Collins, eds. *Military Ethics and Professionalism*. Washington, D.C.: National Defense University Press, 1981. These five essays were initially prepared for a conference held at the Air University (Maxwell Air Force Base, Alabama) under the sponsorship of the Inter-University Seminar on Armed Forces and Society. They deal with ethical foundations of the military profession, apparent changes in professional military ethics, the misuse of statistics, the moral valuations of professional competence, and the impact of technology on the development of managers and leaders. These essays are good material for service academy, staff college, and war college courses and can be used by instructors in training programs.

3. Bunting, Josiah. *The Lionheads*. New York: Random House, 1971. A fictional account of a unit in Vietnam whose commander faces a number of ethical

issues involving unnecessary risks for his men. An easy-to-read characterization of the careerist concerned about image and promotion as contrasted with the professional whose concern is to win battles with minimum casualties. A good source for student reports.

4. Burns, James MacGregor. *Leadership*. New York: Harper and Row, 1978. An intense, scholarly look at the concept of leadership with sharp focus on the moral dimensions of leadership. Burns introduces an important distinction between "transactional" and "transformational" leadership which is certain to receive much use and additional development and scrutiny. This is an excellent reference for military ethics instructors and for scholars doing research on the ethics of leadership.

5. Department of Defense (DOD Gen–11A). *Code of the U.S. Fighting Force*, 1979. This government pamphlet details the six articles of the Code of Conduct which was initially promulgated by President Eisenhower in 1955. The Code was reaffirmed in a DOD directive in 1964, and again in 1977, when President Carter amended Article V which deals with responses permitted while one is a prisoner of war. Dissemination of the Code to every military member is necessary; this pamphlet is suitable for use in all levels of military ethics instruction.

6. Drisko, Melville A., Jr. *An Analysis of Professional Military Ethics: Their Importance, Development and Inculcation*. Carlisle Barracks, Pa.: U.S. Army War College, 1977. This empirical study, done while LTC Drisko attended the Army War College, explores "the degree to which there is unethical conduct among officers and how the Army deals with it; the effectiveness of training programs on military ethics in Army service schools and units; and the perceived need for mottos and codes as a guide to ethical behavior." The study found strong concern among all officers for military ethics, perceptions that better training programs in professional ethics are needed, and a two-to-one opinion favoring the development of a formalized code. Teachers of military ethics will find this research report useful.

7. Galligan, Francis B. *Military Professionalism and Ethics*. Newport, R.I.: Naval War College Center for Advanced Research, 1979. This study pursues the thesis that the general ethical conduct of military professionals does not meet the standards of professional military ethics. The study involves an intensive search of the literature of contemporary articles and research studies and provides a useful bibliography of these works. It makes a number of recommendations for improving the ethical climate in the services and for better techniques in teaching military ethics. The study will be useful to teachers of military ethics.

8. Girdon, Terry A. *Current Military Values*. Newport, R.I.: Naval War College Center for Advanced Research, 1980. Using Rokeach's five essential categories of values research, Girdon examines the personal values of military officers through the writings of senior military leaders and less senior military scholars; analyzes those officers' perceptions of their organization's values; does a content analysis of some relevant official and semiofficial military publications

dealing with values; makes use of studies done on the values of military academy, ROTC, and OCS cadets (future officers); and summarizes findings concerning military values produced by a wide variety of nonmilitary scholars. Girdon draws from these sources a consensus of nine ideal military values, which he consolidates into four value clusters and then rank orders. Teachers of military ethics will find this study a valuable resource because of its content and the extensive bibliography it presents.

9. Hackett, LTG Sir John Winthrop. *The Profession of Arms*. London: The Times Publishing Co. Limited, 1962. This small collection of General Hackett's Cambridge lectures provides an important perspective on the development of the military profession with special emphasis on its moral dimension. Hackett is a distinguished military professional as well as a significant scholar. The lectures entitled "Society and the Soldier: 1914-18," and "Today and Tomorrow," are especially suited for use in officer training programs and war colleges. (These along with his equally significant 1970 lecture, "The Military in the Service of the State," are reprinted in *War, Morality, and the Military Profession* edited by Wakin).

10. Huntington, Samuel P. *The Soldier and the State*. Cambridge, Mass.: Harvard University Press, 1957. This book is viewed as a classic discussion of U.S. civil-military relations. The first three chapters, which deal with officership as a profession and the professional military ethic, have been anthologized frequently and have been the subject of a number of critical articles. They comprise excellent material for discussion in any military ethics course.

11. Janowitz, Morris. *The Professional Soldier*. New York: The Free Press, 1960 and 1970. Like Huntington's *The Soldier and the State*, Janowitz's work is viewed as a classic study of the U.S. military profession. But unlike Huntington's, Janowitz's book is an empirical study of the evolutionary development of military organizations and leadership. It is a critical resource for any teacher of military ethics and contains several chapters suitable for student reading assignments and discussion.

12. Johnson, Dewey E., ed. *Concepts of Air Force Leadership*. Gunter Air Force Base, Ala.: Air University (Air Force ROTC), 1970. Some of the articles included in chap. 4 of this large anthology are not readily available elsewhere and hence chap. 4 serves as a resource for teachers of military ethics. The volume was prepared for use in Air Force ROTC programs and the articles are suitable for student reading assignments and discussion.

13. Kemble, C. Robert. *The Image of the Army Officer in America*. Westport, Conn.: Greenwood Press, 1973. This study of the development of the U.S. military profession and civil-military relations provides useful insights for military ethics instructors. One of its theses is that American attitudes toward military professionals are complex and are constantly being revised. The author sees a particular identity crisis for the U.S. military professional in the 1970s and looks to society as a whole for the resolution of that crisis.

14. Marshall, S.L.A. *The Armed Forces Officer* (DOD Gen-36). Washington, D.C.: U.S. Government Printing Office, 1975. This latest paperback edition constitutes a complete revision of a classic manual, first issued in 1950. It has been used by service academy and ROTC instructors over the years, and a number of chapters are relevant for courses in military ethics. It seems best suited for use in the precommissioning programs and junior officer professional courses.

15. Myrer, Anton. *Once an Eagle*. New York: Holt, Rinehart and Winston, 1968 (Berkley Medallion, 1976). This novel is included here because its principal characters exemplify graphically both desirable and undesirable moral conduct and traits of military professionals. The contrast between the solid professional hero and the ego-oriented careerist provides excellent material for class discussion. The book would be suitable for student reports in a military ethics course of reasonable duration.

16. Sheehan, Neil. *The Arnheiter Affair*. New York: Random House, 1971. The real-life story of Navy Commander Marcus Aurelius Arnheiter, as told by *New York Times* writer Neil Sheehan, so resembles fictional events in *The Caine Mutiny* that parallels are unavoidable. The many lessons to be learned about careerism and officership from this work make it an excellent resource for military ethics instructors and a good book to assign for student reports.

17. Smith, Tommy D. and George H. Updegrove, eds. *Officership*. Maxwell Air Force Base, Ala.: Air War College (ATC), 1981. Many of the readings in this locally produced anthology are relevant and useful at the staff college and war college level for military ethics courses. Several of the articles may be found in other collections, but several have not been anthologized elsewhere, making this an additional useful resource.

18. U.S. Army Ethics Task Force. *Ethics and Professionalism*. Fort Benjamin Harrison, Ind.: U.S. Army Support Center, 1981. This volume is an instructor guide to a twelve-lesson course on professional military ethics. It contains a list of goals, an approach to moral decisionmaking (shown in the form of a model), detailed lesson plans, additional instructor references, case studies, and tips for instructors on dealing with each topic. It is a very useful reference for military ethics instructors at every level. The materials for each lesson are well selected, but it is doubtful that evan a master teacher could do justice to the quantity of material suggested for each fifty-minute lesson. Adaptations of this course could work well for ROTC students (its intended audience), OTS, branch schools, and junior officer professional schools (e.g., Squadron Officer's School).

19. U.S. Army War College. *Readings on Professionalism*. Carlisle Barracks, Pa.: U.S. Army War College, 1980. This locally produced anthology of articles on professionalism was edited by COL Paul W. Child, Jr., and its thirty-five articles make it one of the largest collections devoted to professionalism and professional military ethics currently available. It is an extremely valuable source for instructors and easily adaptable for student readings and discussion.

Copyright restrictions, however, limit the latter sort of use outside the Army War College as is the case with several other locally printed anthologies.

20. U.S. Army War College. *Study on Military Professionalism*. Carlisle Barracks, Pa.: U.S. Army War College, 1970. This is a landmark study, recently reissued, of significant value to every person interested in professional military ethics. It highlights the perceived difference between the actual operating values of the Army Officer Corps and stated professional ideals. It makes several recommendations for major changes in institutional policies that could bring actual conduct closer to the ideal ethical standards. This is an extremely important resource, especially for use at the senior service schools.

21. Vagts, Alfred. *A History of Militarism*. New York: The Free Press, Rev. Ed., 1959. In this classic study, Vagts wages a relentless battle against "militarism" which he distinguishes from "the military way." He traces the development of militarism from feudal to contemporary times, revealing in the process the roots of the concept of the "gentleman" officer. This work can be extremely useful as an instructor or student reference, especially for the historical background it provides, although it is not easily used as a student text.

22. Wakin, Malham M., ed. *War, Morality, and the Military Profession*. Boulder, Colo.: Westview Press, 1979. This may be the only available text that provides readings on the role of ethics in the military profession and on the difficult issues of war and morality within the same volume. It is used in ethics courses and military studies courses at the U.S. Air Force Academy and in the recently developed Army ROTC military ethics course. It is a valuable resource for any program in professional military ethics.

23. Wolfe, Malcolm E., et al., eds. *Naval Leadership*. Annapolis, Md.: United States Naval Institute, Second Edition, 1959. This leadership text, oriented toward the development of naval officers, gives special attention to moral leadership, placing responsibility for moral guidance and example on the shoulders of the line officer in command.

24. Wouk, Herman. *The Caine Mutiny*. Garden City, N. Y.: Doubleday, 1952. This well-known novel from the era of the Second World War depicts with acute empathy the moral quandaries of junior officers concerned about the possible incompetence of their commander. Wouk provides an important opportunity for reflection on the difficulty of moral decisionmaking in the hierarchical military context, presenting the issues with realistic ambiguity in a way that engages the reader's emotions. This novel would be an excellent subject for student reports.

B. War and Morality

1. Clancy, William, ed. *The Moral Dilemma of Nuclear Weapons*. New York: The Council on Religion and International Affairs, 1961. A series of ten essays

including papers by John Courtney Murray, Walter Millis, and Paul Ramsey. The essayists take issue with each other, providing an important dialogue in presenting the moral issues associated with modern warfare.

2. Cohen, M., Nagel, T., and Scanlon, T., eds. *War and Moral Responsibility*. Princeton, N.J.: Princeton University Press, 1974. Eight essays selected from the first two volumes of the journal *Philosophy and Public Affairs*. The authors deal with fundamental moral justifications for actions in war, as well as with specific issues generated during World War II and the Vietnam War.

3. Fagothy, Austin, S.J. *Right and Reason*. 6th Ed. St. Louis: C.V. Mosby Co., 1976. This work is listed here specifically for chap. 36, "War," which is noted for the clarity with which Fagothy applies and reinterprets classic just war theory to modern warfare.

4. McWilliams, Wilson C. *Military Honor After My Lai*. New York: The Council on Religion and International Affairs, 1972. This brief work includes commentaries on McWilliams' essay by Josiah Bunting, David Little, and William V. O'Brien. It raises several of the issues regarding "military necessity" and war crimes.

5. Nagle, William J., ed. *Morality and Modern Warfare*. Baltimore: Helicon Press, 1960. Eight articles on the morality of nuclear warfare, accompanied by a lengthy bibliography of articles on this issue, mostly written in the 1950s.

6. O'Brien, William V. *Nuclear War, Deterrence and Morality*. Westminster, Md.: Newman Press, 1967. A thorough examination of the complexity of applying just war theory to modern war.

7. Peers, William R., LTG *The Peers Report*. vol. I, Washington, D.C.: U.S. Government Printing Office, 1970. A detailed account of the events that occurred at My Lai on March 16, 1968. General Peers and his team of investigators carefully gathered information implicating American soldiers in the massacre of a large number of noncombatants. Conclusions were drawn in this report that questioned the adequacy and competence of Army leadership at several levels, and overt attempts to suppress information. Recommendations were made to investigate several officers and enlisted men for numerous serious violations of the law of war and the Uniform Code of Military Justice. This report is an excellent resource for instructors who deal with the issues of unlawful or immoral orders, integrity in reporting, and obligations regarding the laws of war.

8. Rains, Roger A., and Michael J. McRee, eds. *The Proceedings of the War and Morality Symposium*. West Point, N.Y.: U.S. Military Academy, 1980. This pamphlet collects the remarks of Brandt, Nagel, Walzer, Lewy, and Taylor, among others delivered at a symposium exploring morality and nuclear warfare, individual responsibilities in war, and the morality of military intervention. Several sections have been reprinted, with the authors' permission, in *Parameters*.

9. Taylor, Telford. *Nuremberg and Vietnam: An American Tragedy*. Chicago: Quadrangle Books, Inc., 1970 (Bantam edition, 1971). A concise treatment of classic just war theory, war crimes, and the issues surrounding superior orders involving illegal or immoral activity.

10. Tucker, Robert W. *Just War and Vatican Council II: A Critique*. New York: The Council on Religion and International Affairs, 1966. This booklet includes commentaries on Tucker's views by George C. Higgins, Ralph Potter, Richard H. Cox, and Paul Ramsey. Tucker argues that there is no way of reconciling the principle that evil may not be done or threatened to bring about a good end with the fundamental necessities of the statecraft of a nuclear power.

11. Tucker, Robert W. *The Just War*. Baltimore: The Johns Hopkins Press, 1960. A critical analysis of the view that in contemporary times the only morally acceptable condition ("just cause") for waging war is self-defense.

12. Rachels, James. *Moral Problems*, 2nd Ed. New York: Harper and Row, 1975. Section 6 of this anthology on a number of moral problems includes four representative articles on morality and war written by Anscombe, Wasserstrom, Lackey, and Narveson.

13. Ramsey, Paul. *War and the Christian Conscience*. Durham, N.C.: Duke University Press, 1961. A frequently referenced discussion of a Christian approach to the classic issues of war and morality.

14. Wakin, Malham M., ed. *War, Morality, and the Military Profession*. Boulder, Colo.: Westview Press, 1979. Part 2 of this anthology includes an introduction by the editor and sixteen articles by contemporary authors on the morality of war and morality in war.

15. Walzer, Michael. *Just and Unjust Wars*. New York: Basic Books, Inc., 1977. Subtitled, "A Moral Argument with Historical Illustrations," this detailed analysis of Walzer's is well worth the time and reflection required to work through it. He contrasts "human rights" arguments with "utilitarian" positions, using historical examples to illustrate which wars are or are not justified by his criteria. He provides a "theory of aggression," derives the rights of states from those of citizens, and deals with the issues of noncombatant status in modern war, the principle of double effect, guerrilla war, terrorism, reprisals, and "military necessity," The book is one of the most useful treatments presently available.

16. Wasserstrom, Richard A. *War and Morality*. Belmont, Calif.: Wadsworth Publishing Co., 1970. This paperback anthology contains eight major articles including William James' "The Moral Equivalent of War" and contemporary essays by Anscombe, Ford, Walzer, Narveson, Lewy, and Wasserstrom.

17. United States Air Force Pamphlet 110–31, *International Law—The Conduct of Armed Conflict and Air Operations*. Washington, D.C.: U.S. Government Printing Office, 1976. This pamphlet summarizes many of the international

law requirements applicable during armed conflicts, with special attention to air operations.

18. United States Air Force Pamphlet 110–34, *Commander's Handbook on the Law of Armed Conflict*. Washington, D.C.: U.S. Government Printing Office, 1980. "This pamphlet informs commanders and staff members of their rights and duties under the law of armed conflict."

19. United States Army Field Manual 27–10, *The Law of Land Warfare*. Washington, D.C.: U.S. Government Printing Office, 1956 (includes certain changes added in 1976). A comprehensive presentation of relevant treaty provisions and statutes binding upon the U.S. armed forces during armed hostilities.

C. Journals

1. *Air University Review*. Professional journal of the U.S. Air Force published at Maxwell Air Force Base, Ala. Frequently includes articles on military ethics.

2. *Armed Forces and Society*. Interdisciplinary journal of the Inter-University Seminar on Armed Forces and Society. Published by Sage Publications, Inc., Beverly Hills, Calif. Occasionally includes articles on military ethics.

3. *Ethics*. An international journal of social, political, and legal philosophy. Published by the University of Chicago Press. Occasionally includes articles on morality and war.

4. *Naval War College Review*. Journal of the Naval War College, published in Newport, R.I. Frequently includes articles on military ethics.

5. *Parameters*. Journal of the Army War College, published at Carlisle Barracks, Pa. Frequently includes articles on military ethics.

6. *Philosophy and Public Affairs*. Princeton University Press. Occasionally includes articles on morality and war.

7. *United States Air Force Academy Journal of Professional Military Ethics*. Published at the USAF Academy, Colorado. All articles devoted to military ethics.

D. Organizations

1. *The Hastings Center* (360 Broadway, Hastings-on-Hudson, N.Y. 10706). Maintains materials on professional ethics, including professional military ethics. Sponsors national workshops on professional ethics, which include military ethics as a substantial area of consideration.

2. *Inter-University Seminar on the Armed Forces and Society* (Box 46, 1126 East 59th Street, Chicago, Il. 60637). This interdisciplinary, international organ-

ization was established more than twenty years ago at the University of Chicago with Morris Janowitz as its founding chairman. Its membership includes civilian and military scholars from many disciplines and from many countries. It sponsors a number of regional meetings each year and a national meeting in Chicago every two years. Papers, topics of discussion, and publications frequently deal with military ethics.

3. *Joint Service Conference on Professional Ethics (JSCOPE)*. Formally organized by ethics instructors from several armed services of the U.S. in January, 1980, after an informal meeting the previous year. Its purpose is to assist military ethics instructors with substantive materials and teaching innovations and to provide a forum for dialogue on military ethics issues. The group meets annually in January, with different military organizations acting as hosts, and publishes the proceedings for members. Administrative matters are handled by Colonel Malham M. Wakin, Department of Philosophy and Fine Arts, USAF Academy, Colo. 80840.

E. A Handful of Readers in Ethical Theory

The following brief list is provided only as a suggested place to start for those seeking introductory level readings on the various ethical theories that might provide a background for or comprise a substantial portion of a professional military ethics course. There are many, many ethics texts available; those listed are merely a small sample.

1. Albert, E.M., T.C. Denise, and S.P. Peterfreund, eds. *Great Traditions in Ethics*, 4th Ed. New York: D. Van Nostrand Co., 1980.

2. Baier, Kurt. *The Moral Point of View*. Ithaca, N.Y.: Cornell University Press, 1958.

3. Brandt, Richard B., ed. *Value and Obligation*. New York: Harcourt, Brace and World, Inc., 1961.

4. Ewing, A.C. *Ethics*. New York: The Free Press, 1953.

5. Johnson, Oliver A., ed. *Ethics: Selections from Classical and Contemporary Writers*, 4th Ed. New York: Holt, Rinehard and Winston, 1978.

6. Melden, A.I., ed. *Ethical Theories: A Book of Readings*, 2nd Ed. Englewood Cliffs, N.J.: Prentice-Hall, Inc., 1967.

7. Oldenquist, Andrew C. *Moral Philosophy: Text and Readings*, 2nd Ed. Boston: Houghton Mifflin Co., 1978.

8. Taylor, Paul W. *Principles of Ethics: An Introduction*. Belmont, Calif. Wadsworth Publishing Co., 1975.